String Fling

Scrappy, happy and loving it!

Bonnie K. Hunter

String Fling

Scrappy, happy and loving it!

By Bonnie K. Hunter

Editor: Jenifer Dick
Designer: Brian Grubb
Photography: Aaron T. Leimkuehler
Illustration: Eric Sears
Technical Editor: Kathe Dougherty
Production Assistance: Jo Ann Groves

Bonnie K. Hunter
Website: www.quiltville.com
Email: quiltville@gmail.com

Published by:
Kansas City Star Books • 1729 Grand Blvd.
Kansas City, Missouri, USA 64108

First edition, ninth printing
ISBN: 978-1-61169-047-7

Library of Congress Control Number: 2012936210

Printed in the United States of America by Wals-
worth Publishing Co., Marceline, MO

Kansas City Star Quilts is an imprint of
C&T Publishing, Inc., P.O. Box 1456,
Lafayette, CA 94549. ctpub.com

PickleDish.com
The Quilter's Home Page

KANSAS CITY STAR QUILTS
Continuing the Tradition

*We would like to thank McFarland Custom
Builders and Reece and Nichols for allowing
us to take our photos at their model home at
Woodneath Farms, a Hunt Midwest Communi-
ty. It was such a wonderful venue for showing
off the quilts to perfection. Thank you! www.
HuntMidwest.com*

Dedication

This book is for all of my quilter friends, who live with, and even sometimes love my little quirks – like my habit of digging through everyone's trash bins after hours on retreat to scavenge up every usable piece, knowing full well I'll never be able to sew it all up even if I had several lifetimes in which to attempt it! You lift me when I'm down, you comfort me when I'm stressing out over things I have no control over. Your words of wisdom speak peace to my soul and remind me to JUST BREATHE! You join me for lunches and sew-a-thons when my schedule allows, and you understand when it doesn't. Your phone calls and emails keep me connected to home. You are the sisters of my heart.

And for my family, my rock, my foundation. Thank you for encouraging me to reach for my dream every day, and not minding – too much – if we end up with grilled cheese and canned tomato soup for dinner once too often.

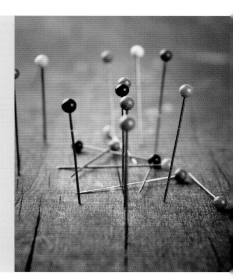

Acknowledgements

String Fling is my fourth Kansas City Star book – and the years are flying by. I am as excited about this book as I was my first, when we released **Scraps & Shirttails** in fall 2008. **Adventures with Leaders & Enders** was released in spring 2010, being closely followed by **Scraps & Shirttails II** in spring 2011. I've been lucky! SO LUCKY! I've been able to keep much of the same staff through each book release, and the process of moving from one project to the next has been continual, seamless, and easy. Simply said, I work with the best group of people on the planet, and each and every one of you deserves my gratitude tenfold.

Of course, I have to begin – as always – with my immediate family. As this goes to print, Dave and I are close to celebrating our 31st anniversary. How can that be possible when I certainly don't feel that old! Our two boys are grown and thriving in their own lives, and I am so proud of the wonderful men they have become, and are continually growing to be. I couldn't do any of this without their support and understanding. Thank you, Dave, Jason, Jeff – I love you!

2012 also marks the year I turned 50. I'm so happy to have this book to celebrate my milestone!
My complete and heartfelt thanks go to the staff at Kansas City Star Books – we've done it again thanks to all of you. Special thanks to Doug Weaver and Diane McLendon for continuing to believe in my dream of putting my quilts in print to share with all of you. Together, we may just make a dent in sewing up the scraps into the best quilts of our lives!

I'd like to thank the team that helped me put this book together: Brian Grubb, Aaron Leimkuehler, Kathe Dougherty, Jo Ann Groves and Eric Sears. Special thanks to Jenifer Dick, for fitting me into her busy schedule a fourth time, in between writing her own Kansas City Star books and being a busy mom herself. Thanks for being a friend, Jenifer!

Remember, if it's still UGLY, you just didn't cut it SMALL ENOUGH –

Bonnie K Hunter

Foreward

Scraps! We've all got them – big pieces, small pieces – some we've saved from our own projects, others we've acquired from other quilter-friends who know of our love and passion for great variety in our quilts. I've always said, once you go scrappy, you never go back!

For me, there is great satisfaction in finding "just the right spot" for that one little left over bit, sewing it into the block, into the quilt, watching it become part of a beautiful whole.

Just as an artist works with canvas and paint, I think of every string added to each string block as a brush stroke of color, a bit of texture and contrast. Standing alone, by itself, a string may not be much to look at, but when joined with a multitude of other also seemingly unusable and humble pieces, they create a symphony of exciting beauty and unlimited possibility.

The 13 string-based quilts in this book are sure to whet your appetite for digging into your scraps and creating your own unique, one-of-a-kind string quilts, for each string quilt is unique – there are no two alike ever! Even when made in the same design, simply the fact that the fabrics vary so much quilter by quilter, it is impossible to duplicate a string quilt.

I have to thank internet quilter-friends near and far who knew of my penchant for little pieces and strings, often filling "flat rate" boxes with their own treasures and sending them to me anonymously – sometimes with no return address attached! I accepted the challenge – if you look close enough, you just might find your scraps in these quilts – long may they live!

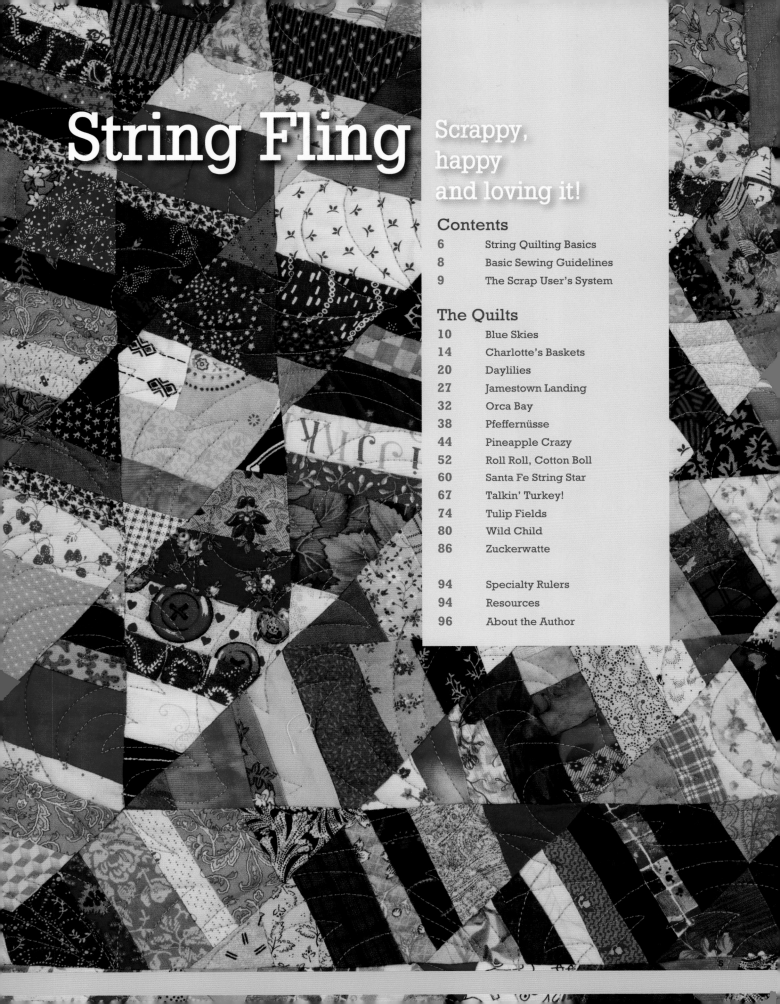

String Fling

Scrappy, happy and loving it!

Contents

String Quilting Basics

Small strips of fabric, little bits of cloth – every color of the rainbow. Each piece a reminder of quilts created, and given in love. Sometimes these small strips or "strings" are the only bit left from the fabrics that have passed through our lives as quilters. It never ceases to amaze me that I can hold the smallest, most insignificant piece in my hands and suddenly I am transported back in time. I know where that fabric came from. I remember vividly the quilt that it was used in.

These scraps and pieces are a connection to my memories, the fabric of my life. Some people mark their lives by the music or the fashions of the day – "Oh, I remember this song. This was when I was in high school." Fabric is my music. Each changing colorway and trend a spot on the time line of my life.

What is a String?

Historically, the term "string" came to be used to define a piece of fabric that was "too small" to be used in household sewing. Too small for clothing construction, too small for household linens – these were the bits destined for the trash bins. In most cases, they were too small to even be considered as rags.

But quilters are and always have been a resilient lot, and of course we could find a use for them. Patterns emerged, and with sewing the strips to a foundation of paper or fabric, these strings found places of beauty in stunning quilts from the most humble of circumstances.

String quilts have always fascinated me – the randomness of placement, the variety of color – and most of all the stories these quilts and fabrics could tell about their makers – if only quilts could talk.

Though many string quilts were simply considered to be utilitarian quilts in nature, they hold a charm and a vibrant freedom that many other traditionally pieced quilts do not have.

Make just one string quilt, and you will find out why!

In this book, I've combined my love of strings together with recognizable traditional patchwork elements. String units mixed with other patchwork pieces add a dynamic eye-catching feature in a scrap quilt!

How Wide Are Strings?

In modern terms, a string is any narrow piece of fabric from about 2″ wide, narrowing down to ¾″ wide.

2″ is pushing the limits in my book, and I prefer to sew with narrower strips simply because I enjoy the variety and the play of the different fabrics when there are more in my blocks. ¾″ is the narrowest I'd use because with ¼″ seams on both sides, there has to be a minimum of ¼″ showing after it is sewn. I love to vary the sizes of my strips, and find it fun to even lay things at a slight angle from time to time to change the direction of the strings so they are not all marching in a straight orderly row like little soldiers. Let them play, let them dance! Take a walk on the wonky side!

Let's Talk About Foundations.

The reason we want to use a foundation is two-fold.

1. A foundation stabilizes the block when working with narrow strips, especially when the strips may be slightly off grain, or not have straight edges.

2. A foundation gives me a boundary to shoot for! I know the size of my block, and if the strip will fit or not. I can very effectively use my scraps to fill the block dimensions this way.

In looking at vintage quilts, you will find any and every fabric used for foundations in string piecing – muslin, printed cotton, batiste, lawn and many others. In the paper foundation category, I've seen everything used – sheet music, church bulletins, newspaper and even family letters.

I prefer to use paper foundations in my string piecing for many reasons. One reason is that I find that sewing straight strips of fabric across the bias of a fabric foundation can cause warping and rolling and a foundation that won't lay flat. Paper is sturdy in every direction, making my results consistent every time.

Another reason I choose to use a paper foundation for my string piecing is because I want to be able to remove the paper before sewing the units together in the quilt. Many of my quilts are made with lots and lots of little pieces. If I stitched them on a fabric foundation, that is just more bulk to sew into the seams adding more weight to an already heavy quilt top. **Charlotte's Baskets**, found on page 14 was hand quilted. If I had used fabric foundations, the hand quilting would have been murder on me!

In my quilts, my favorite paper to use for the foundation is phone book pages.

In my quilts, my favorite paper to use for the foundation is phone book pages. It is a very light-weight paper, it tears easily and it is abundantly free! Use the oldest phone book you can find so the ink has had a long time to cure. This will keep it from bleeding onto your fabric.

Paper foundations to try:

- Phone book pages
- Doodle pads from the dollar store
- Printer paper. We've all got reject printer paper that we can give one more use to before it hits the trash bin.

What not to use:

- Newspapers. The ink will bleed onto your fabric.
- Vellum. It curls up and shrinks when pressed with a hot iron.

Sewing the Strings

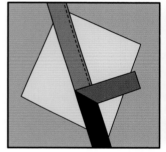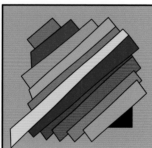

Start by laying two strips right-sides together across the center diagonal of the foundation square. Sew the two pieces together through the paper. Flip the top strip over and press. Do not use steam. Continue adding strips until the entire foundation is covered. Each pattern in this book will give you the size to make the foundations and trimming size to complete the block for each quilt.

Tip: I like to have two blocks going at one time, using each as the "Leader or Ender" for the other. To do this, feed one block through the machine, and without cutting the threads, feed the second block through chaining the first and second block together. Clip the first block off the chain of thread behind the presser foot and without removing the second block from the machine, bring the first block forward and add another piece to it. You can string piece continuously this way, with each block chasing the tail of the other, without any messy long threads all over your sewing area. I find this method even more convenient than stitching a long continuous chain of many blocks that can get tangled up behind my machine.

De-Papering Your Block

Paper removes easily if you remember the following:
- Use a denim needle in your machine to make bigger holes in the paper. (Size 90/14 works great!)
- Remember to set your stitch length very small – on my Bernina I set it at 1.5 or 18-20 stitches per inch.

Smaller stitches and bigger needle holes make that paper easy to remove. If your paper is falling off too soon, lengthen your stitch just a bit. If your stitches are too large, you may find the stitches pulling and distorting when you remove the paper.

I find that paper is hardest to remove when seam lines cross other seam lines. So, in my quilts, I string piece my blocks, square them up and remove the paper right then and there before sewing the units together in the quilt. Once my units are pieced and squared up and de-papered, I can simply sew them together in the quilt just like any other pieced block.

Blocks will have bias edges so handle them carefully. Some might find it helpful to use spray starch on the block before squaring up and removing the paper to add some stiffness to the block.

To remove the paper from the block, fold one corner down along the stitching line, and then working as if you were tearing a piece of paper from a school notebook, grasp just the one piece, and remove it from left to right along the seam. Loosen the edge of the next strip of paper from the seam line, fold it back along the seam line below it, and remove it in the same way. Paper should come off easily. I find if I hold my thumb nail on the beginning of the stitching line, those stitches will stay secure as I remove the paper.

Basic Sewing Guidelines

The patterns for the quilts in this book are based on rotary cutting and machine piecing methods, with some hand appliqué involved, as in the **Daylilies** quilt found on page 20. It is assumed that the reader has a basic knowledge of quilting techniques and processes. The tools used are also the same as in basic quiltmaking. To avoid frustration, it is necessary to have a sewing machine in good working order. Only a straight stitch is required. There are a few additional tips I've picked up along the way to make my quilt making easier and faster and I'd like to share them with you.

That ¼″ seam allowance

It is important to find where the ¼″ seam is on your machine. If you can master this, all your blocks will be the same size and you'll be able to match points perfectly. Even if your machine foot has a ¼″ seam guide on it, it is easy to over-shoot your ¼″ seam by pushing your fabric too hard up against that guide. Do a seam and test it. Do not trust any feet with "built in" guides until you do!

Feet with built-in guides are good for running along the edge of patchwork pieces, but when string piecing on foundations, you may have better luck with a foot without a guide, as guided feet don't like to sew "cross-country" well! A basic foot with an open toe is all that is required for string piecing as seam allowance is not as crucial on these blocks. We just need a straight seam – it doesn't have to be a perfect ¼″ for the string blocks. You might find yourself string piecing with one foot, and doing the regular patchwork parts with your ¼″ guided foot.

Chain piecing with Leaders & Enders

Continuous chain piecing is not a new concept, and quilters have been doing it for years. By aligning fabric patches, right sides together before sewing, you can feed the fabric pairs through the machine one after another without stopping. This saves a ton of thread!

It is through the years, however that I have evolved the process of chain piecing with Leaders & Enders to make, in essence, two quilts at once!

Traditionally a scrap of fabric folded in half is used to start off and finish the line of chain pieced patches, with the main work being snipped off from behind the presser foot, leaving the folded over scrap held in place by the machine needle under the foot. This keeps the thread from bunching up underneath the first patch sewn in the line. Over time, I realized that the little scrap of fabric with its mess of thread was still being thrown away. Now I use pre-cut pairs of squares or other shapes such as half-square triangles as the Leaders & Enders, instead of the thread covered scrap. These pieces will become units for another quilt, or fit into the quilt I am currently working on.

You can learn more about chain piecing with Leaders & Enders in my book, **Adventures with Leaders & Enders**. Ask for it at your local quilt shop or go to my website, Quiltville.com to order.

Pressing

I like to press with a dry iron (no steam). If I feel the area I'm pressing can use the help of steam, I'll spritz it from a water bottle and press. I also find myself doing a lot of finger pressing, and only pressing the block with the iron when it is completed.

String blocks can be especially stretchy with their trimmed edges revealing the bias of the fabric strips, so pressing with spray starch or some Best Press can help stabilize these areas if you are worried about stretching.

The Scrap User's System

As a long-time scrap quilter, I needed a method that would help keep my scraps readily available for ease in making scrap quilts. I much prefer to be sitting and sewing than pressing and cutting from odd sizes of scraps! If I could tackle the left over scraps from each project as I made them, they'd be ready for me to sew any time I had time.

Along with the string units in the quilts in this book, you will find that the other "patchwork" elements use common sizes of strips. These are sizes of strips we use all the time in traditional patchwork. These all came from my own Scrap User's System of storing strips in useable sizes so they are ready to go. By pre-cutting my scraps and storing them by size and value, I have the ease of pulling the perfect size and color so I can just sit and sew. It's a scrap user's dream!

Scrap Strip Sizes

While the definition of a string is anything from ¾″ to 2″, the sizes of pre-cut strips for my scrap stash is a bit more defined.

I cut fabric pieces that are at least 12″ long into 1 ½″, 2″, 2 ½″ and 3 ½″ widths. I don't cut new yardage this way, just the scraps that are left over from whatever I am working on.

These strips are stored by color and value in plastic drawers that live under the table side of my longarm quilting machine.

I spent the entire month of December 2011 organizing my strips which were already sorted by width to also include sorting by color family as well in an effort to make things more manageable. This might seem extreme to some, but it works for me. For example, I easily pulled the bag of 2 ½″ blue strips and the bag of 2 ½″ neutral strips from the 2 ½″ drawers and easily set about making the half square triangles for **Jamestown Landing** found on page 29. Before I sorted them by color, I was digging through everything just to find the color I was searching for.

Smaller fabric pieces and short strips less than 12″ in length are cut into squares and bricks by the size of the strip.

- 1 ½″ squares and 1 ½″ x 2 ½″ bricks
- 2″ squares and 2″ x 3 ½″ bricks
- 2 ½″ squares and 2 ½″ x 4 ½″ bricks
- 3 ½″ squares

Anything that is too small or oddly shaped to work as a pre-cut strip is delegated to my string bins. And that is how my string bins grew!

As you develop your own system, you will discover what sizes you like to work with and incorporate those into your own Scrap User's System. Always be on the lookout for how you can use your seemingly unusable scraps and cut them into that size and shape ahead of time. Tackle the scraps as you make them. Soon you'll have a sewing room full of organized scraps that are ready to go when you are!

Blue Skies

Blue Skies

FINISHED QUILT SIZE: 84″ SQUARE
FINISHED BLOCK SIZE: 10″

Separating my collection of strings into color families – pulling blues and yellows with a few whites and creams thrown in to lighten and brighten – was the starting point for this quilt. It reminded me of a beautiful sunrise on a bright summer morning. The strings are pieced into yellow and blue blocks, and each color block is strategically sliced and matched with an opposite color to form the block centers.

Fabric Requirements

- 5 yards of scraps in a wide variety of blue hues from light to dark. Push the boundaries and pull in turquoise, and even push toward periwinkle!
- 5 yards of scraps in a wide variety of yellow hues from butter to butterscotch! I threw in some whites and creams to bring in a spark.

Note: All of these fabrics can have other colors playing on them. There may be red fire engines on a blue background, but it will still read as blue. There may be green leaves and pink flowers on a yellow background, but it will still read as yellow. Don't think that these have to be tone-on-tone! Look at the background color of the fabric and let it play!

String Pieced Units

Refer to the string piecing instructions on pages 6-9 to prepare 64 – 7 ½″ foundation squares.

Yellow Units

For the yellow units only it is helpful to start with a 2″ strip down the center diagonal of your foundation since we will be sub-cutting these yellow units down the center diagonal. Continue adding strips until the entire foundation is covered. Trim to 7 ½″ square. Make 32.

Diagrams are on page 13.

A

Referring to the diagram, slice the units from corner to corner **through** the center string. Remove paper. Make 64 triangles.

Blue Units

Start covering the foundations by laying two strips right sides together across the center diagonal of the foundation square. Continue adding strips until the entire foundation is covered. Trim to 7 ½″ square. Make 32.

B

Referring to the diagram, slice the units from corner to corner across the strings. Remove paper. Make 64 triangles.

C

To complete the unit, sew a blue triangle to a yellow triangle with right-sides together and stitch. Press toward the yellow. Repeat for all 64 pairs. Trim units to 6 ½″ square.

Half-Square Triangles

Make 1, 188 – 2 ½″ unfinished, finishing at 2″.

I used the Easy Angle Ruler and 2 ½″ strips from my scraps to cut the triangles used for this quilt. The traditional method of using 2 ⅞″ squares is given for those who do not have access to this ruler. Please see section on Using Specialty Rulers found on pages 94-95. You can use any method that gives you a 2 ½″ unfinished half-square triangle unit that finishes at 2″.

From the dark scraps cut 594 – 2 ⅞″ squares.
From the light scraps cut 594 – 2 ⅞″ squares.

Quilt Top Assembly

Referring to the quilt assembly diagram, lay out the blocks in rows with 8 blocks across and 8 blocks down as shown. Be sure to turn the blocks in the correct direction to make the overall pattern emerge.

Borders

Referring to the quilt assembly diagram, and paying attention to which units are left/top or right/bottom, lay out the border units, rotating them as needed to complete the design around the quilt. The 4 remaining half-square triangle units fill in the 4 corners.

Stitch the quilt center into rows. Join the rows to complete the quilt top.

Finishing

Blue Skies was machine quilted in light blue thread with an edge-to-edge design called Flying Paisley by Jodi Beamish of Willow Leaf Studio, Canada. Refer to the resources page for contact information. A blue binding finishes everything just right!

D

Layer the dark squares and light squares with right sides together. Cut from corner to corner once on the diagonal to yield 1,188 matched pairs. Stitch into 1,188 half square triangle units, enough for 64 blocks and the triangle border. Press to the blue and trim the dog ears. Each block requires 16 half-square triangle units. The border that completes the edge of the quilt will use the remaining 164 half-square triangle units.

Triangle Unit Assembly

You will need to make 3 different triangle units for the blocks and sashing. Refer to the diagrams for each and be careful to pay attention to the direction the triangles are pointing.

Side Block Unit
E

Stitch 3 half-square triangle units side by side. Each block uses 2 of these units. Make 128.

Top/Bottom Block Unit and Left/Top Border Unit
F

Stitch 5 half-square triangle units side by side. Each block uses 2 of these units. Make 128 for blocks and 16 for border units.

Right/Bottom Border Unit
G

Stitch 5 half-square triangle units side by side as shown. Make 16 for border units.

Block Assembly

H

Add a side unit to each side of a center string block as shown. Press. Add a top/bottom unit to the top and bottom of each string block. Press. Make 64 blocks.

On the Flip Side!

Too many blocks? I somehow ended up with more than I needed – and didn't find out until they all had their side units attached. They found a fun place here on the back of the quilt!

Blue Skies
Directions At-A-Glance

A

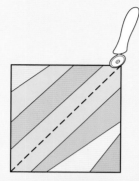

YELLOW STRING UNIT
Make 32 – 7 ½″
unfinished string squares
Cut in half down the center
string to make 64 triangles

B

BLUE STRING UNIT
Make 32 – 7 ½″ unfinished
string squares
Cut in half across the strings
to make 64 triangles

C

STRING PIECED UNIT
6 ½″ unfinished
Make 64

D

HALF-SQUARE TRIANGLE UNIT
2 ½″ unfinished
Make 1,188

E

SIDE BLOCK UNIT
Make 128

F

TOP/BOTTOM BLOCK UNIT AND LEFT/TOP BORDER UNIT
Make 128

G

RIGHT/BOTTOM BORDER UNIT
Make 16

H

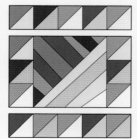

BLOCK ASSEMBLY
10 ½″ unfinished
Make 64

ASSEMBLY DIAGRAM

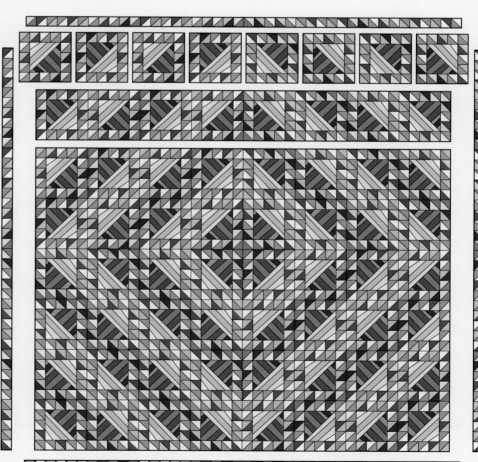

Charlotte's Baskets

FINISHED QUILT SIZE:
APPROXIMATELY 53″ SQUARE

A quick phone call from a friend asking for help in designing a basket block to use her left over bonus triangles resulted in my digging in to make this small quilt! String blocks cut on the diagonal frame each 6″ basket block giving the otherwise ordinary block a vibrant place to play. My love of Pennsylvania Dutch colors takes front stage in the sashing and borders, creating a very happy mix of everything under the sun!

Fabric requirements

1 ½ yards of assorted dark colored scraps for basket triangles, 4-patch cornerstones and strings

1 yard of assorted neutrals/lights for block backgrounds

½ yard of red print for basket base and feet

¾ yard of green solid for sashing

¼ yard cheddar print for inner border

⅔ yard red print for outer border

½ yard black print for binding

Basket Blocks

Small Half-Square Triangle Units

Make 6 per block – 2″ unfinished, finishing at 1 ½″.

I used bonus triangles left over from other projects along with my Easy Angle ruler and 2″ strips to make the half square triangles for this block. The traditional method of using 2 ³⁄₈″ squares is given for those who do not have access to this ruler. Please see section on Using Specialty Rulers found on pages 94-95. You can use any method that gives you a 2″ unfinished half-square triangle unit that finishes at 1 ½″.

From the dark scraps cut 48 – 2 ³⁄₈″ squares.

From the light scraps cut 48 – 2 ³⁄₈″ squares.

Diagrams are on page 19.

A

Layer the dark squares and light squares with right sides together. Cut from corner to corner once on the diagonal to yield 96 matched pairs. Stitch into 96 half-square triangle units, enough for 16 blocks. Press to the dark and trim the dog ears. Each block requires 6 of these scrappy half-square triangle units.

Wing Triangles
B

Cut 16 – 2 ³⁄₈″ squares from light/neutral fabric scraps. Cut these once on the diagonal to yield 32 wing triangles. Each block requires 2 of these.

Basket "Feet"
From the red basket fabric cut 16 – 2 ³⁄₈″ squares

From the light scraps cut 16 – 2 ³⁄₈″ squares.

C

Layer, cut and sew these as above for 32 half square triangle units to be used for basket feet.

Basket Base
I used 3 ½″ strips and my Easy Angle ruler to cut the Basket Base Triangles. If not using this ruler, the traditional method of 3 ⅞″ squares is given.

D

Cut 8 – 3 ⅞″ squares from red basket fabric. Layer these squares and slice once on the diagonal to yield 16 basket base triangles.

Basket Base Assembly

E

Following the diagram, stitch one wing triangle to the two dark sides of 16 half-square triangle units. Press seams toward the wing triangles just added.

Join these units with the basket base units, pressing seam toward the basket triangle.

Block Assembly

Basket Side section 1
F-G

Stitch 2 half-square triangle units side by side. Press seam toward the left triangle. Make 16. Add this unit to the basket center unit. Press seam toward the triangles just added.

Basket side section 2
H-I

Stitch 3 half-square triangle units together as shown. Repeat for all 16 blocks. Press all seams toward the center triangle unit.

Join this unit to the basket center as shown. Press toward the triangles just added.

Basket background and feet
J-K

From light/neutral scraps cut 32 – 2″ x 3 ½″ rectangles. Use 2 for each block.

From light/neutral scraps cut 16 – 2″ squares. Use 1 for each block.

L

Stitch a basket foot unit to the ends of each background rectangle, paying attention to the direction of the triangles. Stitch 16 left side, and 16 right side units as shown. Press toward the background rectangles.

M

Stitch a 2″ background square to each of the left side units. Press toward end square.

N

Stitch the right hand block sides to the block. Press toward the basket.

Add the remaining background section to the block to complete it. Press seam toward the section just added. Make 16 blocks.

String Pieced Frame

Following directions for string blocks on pages 6-9, prepare 35 – 5 ½″ paper foundation squares.

Add strips to either side of the center strip until the paper base is completely covered. Press. Square units to 5 ½″ and remove the paper. Make 32.

O

Slice blocks on the diagonal across the strings, yielding 2 setting triangles from each string block. Make 64.

P

The string pieced corner triangles will be large for the block, but we'll trim later. Center the long edge of a string triangle with the center of one side of the block and stitch it to the block. Repeat for the opposite side. Trim the triangle edges extending beyond the block even with the remaining edges of the block, and add the two remaining string triangles. Press. Repeat for all 16 blocks.

Squaring up

When squaring up the blocks, I use a ruler that has a ¼″ seam line marked all the way around the outside edge of the ruler. You are going to want a large square ruler to do this.

If you are a "righty" place the ¼″ seam line on the ruler on the top corner of the center basket, and slide it so the seam line on the right side is also up against the right side basket corner. Trim up the right side and across the top.

If you are a "lefty" you are going to work from the left instead of the right. Now rotate the block, and trim the two remaining sides this way, leaving ¼″ beyond the 4 basket corners.

Sashing

4-Patch Cornerstones

From scrap fabrics, cut 100 – 1 ½″ squares, and arrange them by color family into a variety of 4-patch units. Mix and match as desired. I used blacks, blues, browns, greens, pinks, purples, reds, and yellows. The quilt requires 25 – 4-patch units that measure 2 ½″ square, and finish at 2″. Make 3 of each color way, plus one extra of whatever color you choose.

Sashing Strips

Measure blocks to determine the average size. Cut strips this length from sashing fabric, sub-cutting the strips into 40 – 2 ½″ x the size of your block.

Referring to the Quilt Assembly Diagram on page 19, lay out the blocks in rows along with the sashings and cornerstones as shown. Stitch the quilt center into rows, pressing seams toward the sashing, and away from the cornerstones. Join the rows to complete the quilt center.

Borders

Inner Border

Cut 5 – 1 ½″ strips across the width of the fabric from selvage to selvage. Join the 5 border strips end to end with diagonal seams to make a strip approximately 200″ long. Trim excess ¼″ from seams and press seams open.

Lay the quilt center out on the floor, smoothing it gently. Do not tug or pull. Measure the quilt through the center from top to bottom. Cut two inner side borders this length. Sew the inner side borders to the quilt sides with right sides together, pinning to match centers and ends. Ease where necessary to fit. Press seams toward the borders.

Repeat for top and bottom inner borders, measuring across the quilt center, including the borders just added in the measurement. Cut top and bottom inner borders this length. Stitch the top and bottom inner borders to the quilt center, pinning to match centers and ends, easing where necessary to fit. Press seams toward borders.

Outer Border

From red print, cut 5 – 4″ strips across the width of the fabric from selvage to selvage. Join the 5 border strips end to end on the straight of grain to make a strip approximately 200″ long. Press seams open.

Add the outer borders in the same manner as the inner borders were added.

Finishing

Charlotte's Baskets was hand quilted in a hoop as I traveled all over the USA. I used red cotton hand quilting thread, and cotton batting. It's a wonderful feeling to rediscover the simplicity of "needle-pulling-thread" through the quilt layers with each stitch. I bound the quilt in a black/green print to finish.

A

HALF-SQUARE TRIANGLE UNITS
1 ½″ unfinished
Make 96

B

WING TRIANGLES
16 – 2 ⅜″ neutral squares cut in half on the diagonal
Make 32

C

BASKET "FEET" HALF-SQUARE TRI-ANGLE UNIT
1 ½″ unfinished
Make 32

D

BASKET BASE
8 – 3 ⅞″ red basket squares cut in half on the diagonal
Make 18

E

BASKET BASE ASSEMBLY
3 ½″ unfinished
Make 16

F

BASKET SIDE SECTION 1 TRIANGLES
Make 16

G

BASKET SIDE SECTION 1
Make 16

H

BASKET SIDE SECTION 2 TRIANGLES
Make 16

I

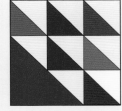

BASKET SIDE SECTION 2
Make 16

J

BACKGROUND RECTANGLE
2″ x 3 ½″ unfinished
Make 32

K

BACKGROUND SQUARE
2″ unfinished
Make 16

L

BASKET BACKGROUND AND FEET
Make 16 each

M

BASKET BACKGROUND AND FEET
Make 16 each

N

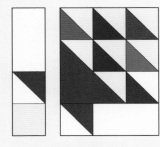

6 ½″ UNFINISHED
Make 16

O

STRING PIECED FRAME
5 ½″ square strings cut in half on the diagonal across the string
Make 64 triangles

P

BASKET BLOCK
Approximately 9″ unfinished
Make 16

ASSEMBLY DIAGRAM

Daylilies

BLOCK SIZE: 14″

QUILT SIZE: APPROXIMATELY 90″ SQUARE

My lily blocks from the 1990s finally found a home! I started these blocks when we still lived in Idaho. They traveled with me through two relocations in Texas, a move to South Carolina and finally to North Carolina. The reason they languished? They were so boring! Every time I laid them out to figure out what to do with them, all I saw was huge amounts of beige background fabric. Of course, laying them out on my beige carpet didn't help matters. They needed color to give them life, and lots of it! They needed updating to bring them into this century, and the wickedly wild string setting blocks gave them just the right place to bloom where they were planted.

The pinwheel border was made with bonus triangle units left from some other quilts – the remainder of which came to live on the back of the quilt.

This quilt does require some careful Y-seaming and a bit of basic appliqué. Because these blocks and pieces are large, this is the perfect quilt to push your skills to a more advanced level.

Fabric Requirements

2 ½ yards of cream tone on tone for block backgrounds

1 ½ yards of green tone on tone for leaves, stems and flower bases

4 yards of colored scraps and strings for Lily blocks, string blocks and pinwheel border

1 ½ yards of assorted neutral/light scrap fabrics for pinwheel border

Additional Supplies Needed

Template plastic

Note: These blocks require Y-seam construction. Please refer to the "Sewing Those Y-Seams!" section on page 61.

Block Cutting

From block background fabric cut:

48 – 2 ½″ squares

16 – 8 ½″ squares

32 – 2 ½″ x 6 ½″ rectangles

24 – 5 ¼″ squares, cut twice with an X to yield 96 setting triangles

From green tone on tone cut:

24 – 4 ½″ squares cut in half on the diagonal to create 48 triangles for flower base triangles (1)

16 - 4 ½″ squares for the block base triangles (2)

Piecing the Lilies

Trace the Diamond Template to template plastic and cut out.

Each Lily block has 3 matching lilies with each consisting of 2 complimentary fabrics with two diamonds cut from each fabric in mirror image. For ease in cutting, cut the scraps for your lilies into 1 ⅞″ strips. Fold the strip with right sides together, and using the template as a guide, cut two diamonds at once.

Cut 3 pairs from each fabric. Repeat for all the diamond pairs for the 16 Lily Blocks.

Diagrams are on pages 25-26.

A

Stitch the diamonds into pairs, and inset each side triangle as shown. Add the corner square. Stitch the base unit (1) to the bottom of the lily. Press. The lily should measure 6 ½″ square unfinished and 6″ finished.

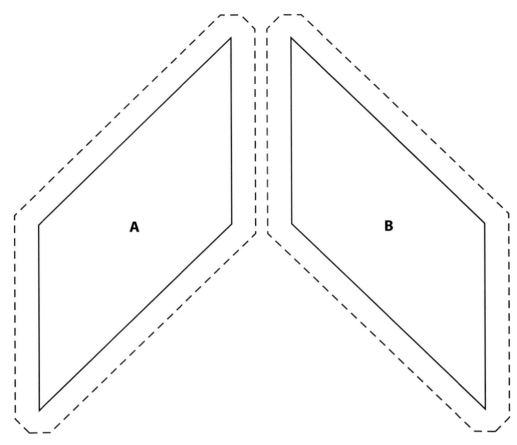

Flower Stem Appliqué

Making Stems

Long bias strips are used for flower stems that bend easily into graceful curves. You can cut bias strips along any 45-degree angle of the grain. To find the bias of the fabric, fold one corner of the fabric down, so that the right side edge of the fabric is even with the bottom edge of the fabric. The FOLD is your bias. Cut along the fold.

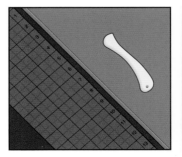 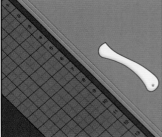

Using a ruler and a hera marker, use the hera marker to make a good crease just under ¼″ from the cut bias edge of the fabric. Make a second crease ⅜″ away from the first.

Finally use your ruler and rotary cutter and cut the fabric just under ¼″ away from the second crease. The fabric will

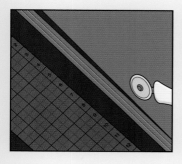

automatically want to fold where you have creased it. Fold both sides of the strip in toward the center of the stem and press with a hot iron. Some spray starch can help you here. Bias strips should be at least 8″ long for ease of use.

Crease the 8 ½″ base block in half on the diagonal for help with stem placement.

B

Following the placement guide, position bias stems in a U shape for the two side flowers and appliqué with your favorite method. If your stem is long enough, you can use one length, or you can use two lengths, positioning the join where the center stem will cover it.

Note: You may want to lay your flower tops next to this block and mark with a pin where the stem is going to join up with the flower base triangle.

Then, appliqué the center stem as shown, extending the top and bottom end of stem at least 2 ½″ from the bottom corner. The base triangle will cover the end of the stem.

Leaf Appliqué

Trace and cut 32 leaves from Freezer paper.

Using a bit of glue stick on the non-shiny side of the paper leaf, stick it to the wrong side of the leaf fabric, and trim a very scant ¼″ all the way around the shape.

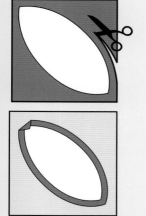

Fold and press the two leaf tips over the shiny side of the freezer paper template.

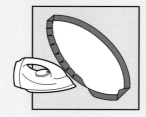

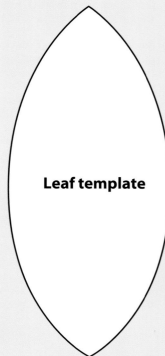

Leaf template

Referring to the diagram, continue pressing the seam allowance around the leaf, clipping curves as needed to get a nice round and smooth edge. Iron the leaf with the paper side down on the block sashings following placement diagram.

Place two leaves on each block as shown and appliqué in place.

Working from the back side of the block, make a small slit in the fabric beneath each leaf, and gently remove the freezer paper, loosening the seam allowance from the paper as you go. Press blocks when done.

Attaching Base Triangle

Draw a line on the back of each square (2) from corner to corner.

Place a square in the bottom of each base block with right sides together as shown. Stitch from corner to corner across the green square following the line. Fold the triangle back to be sure it meets the edge of the base square. Press and trim excess.

Block Assembly

C

Arrange block units as shown and stitch to complete each of the 16 Daylily blocks. Blocks should measure 14 ½″ square unfinished 14″ finished.

String Pieced Units

Referring to the String Piecing directions found on pages 6–9, prepare 48 – 7 ½″ and 16 – 8 ½″ paper foundations.

D

Cover all the foundations with strings using everything-under-the-sun! It is helpful with the 8 ½″ foundations to use a 2″ or wider string down the center, as these will be cut from corner to corner down the length of the center strip.

Trim the 48 small string units to 7 ½″ square and remove the foundation papers.

Trim the 16 large string units to 7 ⅞″ square and slice them on the diagonal down the center strip into 32 string triangles.

Alternate blocks

You will use 36 small string units to make 9 Alternate blocks. The rest will be used to make the Side Setting Triangles.

E

Lay out 4 small string units into an X formation as shown and stitch together to make one block. Repeat to make 9 blocks. The blocks will measure 14 ½″ square unfinished, 14″ finished.

Side Setting Triangles

You will use the 12 remaining small string units and 24 string triangles to make 12 Side Setting Triangles. The remaining 8 will be used to make the Corner Triangles.

F

Stitch a string triangle to adjacent sides of 12 string squares as shown. Press to the triangles.

Corner Triangles

You will use the 8 remaining string triangles to make 4 Corner Triangles.

G

Join 2 triangles side by side into one large corner triangle unit as shown. Press to one side.

Quilt Center Assembly

Daylilies is an "on-point" setting, and assembled in diagonal rows. Referring to the Quilt Assembly Diagram, lay out the blocks and setting squares, filling in the sides with the setting triangles and corners. I like to piece diagonally set quilts into two halves. With this quilt, one "half" will be larger than the other because it is a square quilt! This keeps things from being too unwieldy, especially when sewing a large quilt top. Join quilt top halves to complete quilt center. Press to the Alternate blocks.

At this point your quilt should measure approximately 79 ¾" square. My border units finish at 5" square, and I did a bit of fudging with the seams to get everything to fit the quilt center just right. String piecing and pieced borders are both stretchy, and I find I can either take in a "hair bit more" between the border seams if I need to, or a "hair bit less" just to get things to fit. In this case, I was fudging less than ½" over an 80" border. Not bad, and very doable!

Pinwheel Borders

Pinwheel blocks

These are two-part pinwheels.

Note: I used left over bonus units from other quilts in the pieced pinwheel style border of Daylilies. If you are using the Easy Angle ruler, you can easily cut pieced triangle pairs by sewing 1 ¾" strips together for the pieced side of the unit, and match that strip pieced set with a neutral 3" strip with right sides together. Use the 3" line on the ruler to cut your matched triangle pairs. Border units will measure 3" square and finish at 2 ½" in the quilt. If you aren't using the Easy Angle ruler, use the following directions, but know that you'll have to trim them down after sewing to get the triangles the right size.

From the colored scraps cut, 272 – 2" x 3 ½" rectangles.

From the neutral/light scraps cut, 136 – 3 ½" squares.

H

Sew the 2" rectangles together creating strip pairs measuring 3 ½" square. Press seams to one side.

I

Match neutral squares and strip squares with right sides together. Cut on the diagonal from corner to corner into matched triangle pairs. Stitch the triangle pairs to yield 272 border units. Border units will be a bit over-sized. Trim border units to 3" square, by trimming along the base edges away from the smallest tip triangle. (This small triangle is already small, try not to make it smaller!) Border units will finish at 2 ½" in the quilt.

J

Arrange 4 half-square triangle units as shown to create one border pinwheel. Stitch the units together to form the block. Make 68.

Join 16 border pinwheels into one long unit as shown on the Quilt Assembly Diagram. Make 4 borders this length.

Sew the side borders to the quilt sides with right sides together, pinning to match centers and ends. Ease where necessary to fit. Press seams toward the quilt.

Add a corner pinwheel block to each end of the remaining top and bottom borders. Stitch the top and bottom borders to the quilt center, pinning to match centers and ends, easing where necessary to fit. Press seams toward the quilt.

Finishing

I free-motion quilted **Daylilies** featuring feathers in the pinwheel border and feather motifs in the string blocks using an antique tan colored thread. The lily blocks have feathers in the flower diamonds and curls, swirls and lots of filler texture in the block backgrounds. Even the leaves come to life with some stitching detail quilted in. Flower blocks are quilted with thread to match the fabrics within each block. It just screamed for a purple binding to finish it off.

Daylilies
Directions At-A-Glance

A

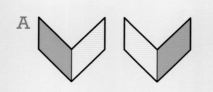

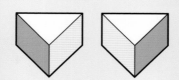

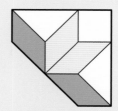

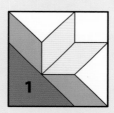

PIECING THE LILIES
Make 3 per block
Make 16 blocks

B

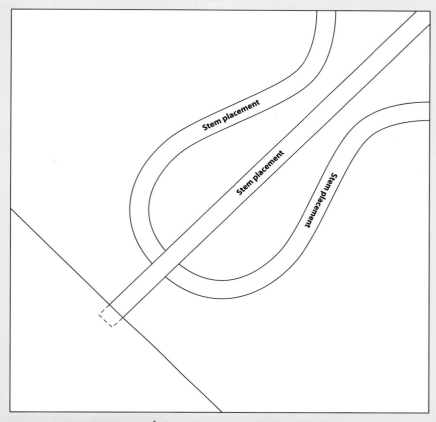

BASE STEM APPLIQUÉ UNIT PLACEMENT GUIDE
8 ½″ unfinished
Make 16

C

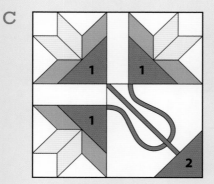

BLOCK ASSEMBLY
14 ½″ unfinished
Make 16

D

STRING PIECED UNITS
Make 48 – 7 ½″ squares (shown left)

Make 16 – 7 ⅞″ squares (shown right).
Cut the 16 - 7 ⅞″ squares in half on the
diagonal with the strings to make 32 setting
triangles.

E

ALTERNATE BLOCKS
14 ½″ unfinished
Make 9

Daylilies
Directions At-A-Glance

F
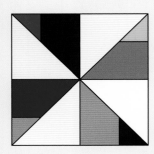

SIDE SETTING TRIANGLES

Make 12

G
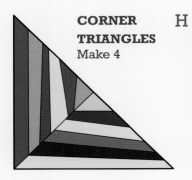

CORNER TRIANGLES

Make 4

H

PINWHEEL BORDER PART 1

3 ½″ unfinished

Make 136

I

PINWHEEL BORDER PART 2

3″ unfinished

Make 272

J

PINWHEEL BORDER BLOCK

5 ½″ unfinished

Make 68

ASSEMBLY DIAGRAM

Jamestown Landing

FINISHED QUILT SIZE: 84″ x 96″

FINISHED BLOCK SIZE: 8″

Stars and chains in blues and neutrals are sure to capture any star-lover's fancy! I love designing projects that will use up every last bit. This quilt was a great way for me to use a large variety of blue and neutral scraps for the half-square triangles, and even more scrap fun clearing out a whole box of neutral strings used in the alternate block areas!

Fabric Requirements

4 yards of blue scraps and strings. Gather a wide variety of prints, stripes, plaids and others ranging in value from light blue to dark navy.

5 yards of light/neutral scraps and strings. Look for a wide variety of prints, stripes and plaids ranging from white to cream to beige to tan. The fabrics may include small figures, leaves and flowers as long as the fabric ground reads as neutral.

¾ yard light/neutral for inner border

Star Blocks

Half-Square Triangle Units

I used the Easy Angle Ruler and 2 ½″ strips from my scraps to cut the triangles used for this quilt. The traditional method of using 2 ⅞″ squares is given for those who do not have access to this ruler. Please see section on Using Specialty Rulers found on pages 94-95. You can use any method that gives you a 2 ½″ unfinished half-square triangle unit that finishes at 2″.

From the blue scraps cut 420 – 2 ⅞″ squares.

From the neutral scraps cut 420 – 2 ⅞″ squares.

Diagrams are on page 30-31.

A

Lay the blue squares and neutral squares right-sides together. Slice diagonally from corner to corner to create 840 matched triangle pairs. Sew triangle pairs with ¼″ seam to yield 840 half-square triangle units. Press seams to the blue fabric and snip the dog ears. Units should measure 2 ½″ unfinished and 2″ finished.

Broken Dishes Units

B

Arrange triangle units as shown to make 210 broken dishes units. Sew together as you would a 4-patch unit, pressing in opposing seams to nest. Unit should measure 4 ½″ unfinished and 4″ finished.

Set aside 46 of the broken dishes units to be used as cornerstones.

Half Star Units

C

Sew the remaining broken dishes into 82 star halves as shown, pressing to one side. Unit should measure 8 ½″ x 4 ½″ unfinished and 8″ x 4″ finished.

Set aside 22 star halves to be used as the outside edges of the quilt center.

D

From the remaining 60 star halves, sew 15 stars with "dark" star points by placing the dark centers together and 15 stars with "light" points by placing the light centers together.

Alternate String blocks

Following directions for string blocks on pages 6-9, prepare 168 – 4 ½″ paper foundation squares.

E

Add strips to either side of the center strip until the paper base is completely covered. Press. Square units to 4 ½″ and remove the paper.

F

Set aside 26 of the string blocks. With the remaining 142 blocks, arrange as shown into pairs and sew into 71 sashing units.

Quilt Assembly

Referring to the Quilt Assembly Diagram on page 31, position the individual broken dishes units, individual string blocks, half stars, string sashing units, and full stars as shown, paying attention to the direction the broken dishes units are pointing to complete the chain effect. Note: The dark pointed stars alternate with light pointed stars, with the light pointed stars in the center of the chains.

Stitch the quilt center into rows and join the rows to complete the quilt center.

Borders

Inner Border

Cut 8 – 2″ strips across the width of the fabric from selvage to selvage. Join the 8 border strips end to end with diagonal seams to make a strip approximately 320″ long. Trim excess ¼″ from seams and press seams open.

Lay the quilt center out on the floor, smoothing it gently. Do not tug or pull. Measure the quilt through the center from top to bottom. Cut two inner side borders this length. Sew the inner side borders to the quilt sides with right sides together, pinning to match centers and ends. Ease where necessary to fit. Press seams toward the borders.

Repeat for top and bottom inner borders, measuring across the quilt center, including the borders just added in the measurement. Cut top and bottom inner borders this length. Stitch the top and bottom inner borders to the quilt center, pinning to match centers and ends, easing where necessary to fit. Press seams toward borders.

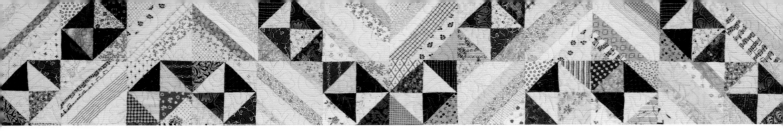

Outer String Border

Cover approximately 16 – 8 ½″ x 11″ pieces of scrap paper with strings running down the length of the page from top to bottom. Short strings can be joined end to end to be long enough to lay the length of the paper. From each string-covered paper, cut 2 – 5″ widths across the page from side to side. Recycled printer paper works great for this. Remove paper from all sections. Join the sections end to end to create one long string pieced border length of approximately 320 inches.

Add the outer borders in the same manner as the inner borders were added.

Finishing

Jamestown Landing was machine quilted in beige thread with an edge to edge design called Harvest Winds by Urban Elementz. Refer to the resources page for contact information. A simple navy binding finishes the edge of the quilt.

Jamestown Landing
Directions At-A-Glance

A

HALF-SQUARE TRIANGLE UNIT
2 ½″ unfinished
Make 840

B

BROKEN DISHES UNIT
4 ½″ unfinished
Make 210

C

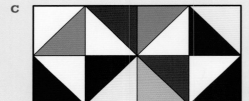

HALF STAR UNIT
8 ½″ x 4 ½″ unfinished
Make 82

D

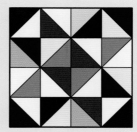 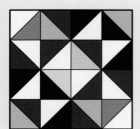

STAR BLOCKS
8 ½″ unfinished
Make 15 each

E

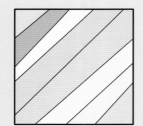

ALTERNATE STRING BLOCK
4 ½″ unfinished
Make 168

F

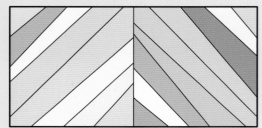

STRING SASHING UNIT
8 ½″ x 4 ½″ unfinished
Make 71

ASSEMBLY DIAGRAM

Orca Bay

Orca Bay

FINISHED QUILT SIZE: 74 ½″ x 84 ½″

FINISHED BLOCK SIZE: 6″

I spent several glorious days with the quilters of Cordova, Alaska in September of 2011. These wonderful women went way out of their way to make sure I had an authentic Alaskan experience, including a trip deep sea fishing in Prince William Sound where Orca Bay is beautiful enough to make me catch my breath. A sunset picture taken from a back deck overlooking the vastness of the water stretching as far as the eye can see inspired me to name this quilt after this most magical of places. I'll always carry Cordova and Orca Bay in my heart!

I had a great time playing with two color families of strings in this quilt. My reds go all the way through the red spectrum from orangey-red to pinky-red to fire engine and everywhere in between. My blues have quite the variety too, from light blue to turquoise and pushing through from royal blue to periwinkle and beyond. I tried to stay away from really dark navy as I didn't want it to make my blacks disappear.

Fabric Requirements

5 yards of light/neutral scraps with a wide variety of prints, stripes, plaids and geometrics ranging from white to cream to beige. Include small figures, leaves and flowers as long as the fabric ground reads as neutral. I avoided anything darker than beige, wanting this quilt to have a lighter feel.

6 yards of black scraps in a wide variety of prints and textures. These also can have other colors playing on them, but have a black background to the fabric.

1 ¼ yard of blue scraps and strings. Gather a wide variety of prints, stripes, plaids, and others ranging in value from light blue to royal blue. Avoid navy fabrics that may be too dark when placed next to black.

3 yards of red scraps and strings in a wide variety of every shade of red. The more the merrier! The more clash the better!

½ yard light/neutral print for the inner border

Hourglass Units

I used the Companion Angle Ruler and 1 ½″ strips from my scraps to cut the quarter-square triangles. The traditional method of using 3 ¼″ squares is given for those who do not have access to this ruler. Please see section on Using Specialty Rulers found on pages 94-95. You can use any method that gives you a 2 ½″ unfinished hour-glass unit that finishes in the quilt at 2″.

From the black scraps cut 112 – 3 ¼″ squares.

From the neutral scraps cut 112 – 3 ¼″ squares.

Layer the black squares and light squares with right sides together. Cut from corner to corner twice on the diagonal with an X to yield 448 matched pairs.

Diagrams are on page 36-37.

A-B

Stitch into 448 half hourglass units, pressing seams toward the black triangles. Join two pairs to create each hourglass unit. Make 224 hourglass units.

From the black scraps cut 112 – 2 ½″ squares

From light/neutral scraps cut 112 – 2 ½″ squares.

From red scraps cut 56 – 2 ½″ squares.

C

Arrange 4 hour glass units, 4 background squares and 1 center square as shown. Stitch units into rows, and join rows to complete each block. Press. Make 28 with black backgrounds, and 28 with light backgrounds.

Wing Triangle Units

I used my Easy Angle Ruler and 2″ strips to cut the small half-square triangles used for this quilt. I also used the ruler and 3 ½″ strips for the larger neutral triangles in this unit. The traditional method of using 2 ⅜″ squares for the small triangles, and 3 ⅞″ squares for the larger triangles is given for those who do not have access to this ruler. Please see section on Using Specialty Rulers found on pages 94-95. You can use any method that gives you a 2″ unfinished half-square triangle unit that finishes at 1 ½″ and a larger unfinished half-square triangle that finishes at 3″.

From black scraps cut 531 – 2 ⅜″ squares.

From light/neutral scraps cut 177 – 2 ⅜″ squares.

D

Lay the 177 light/neutral squares and 177 of the black squares with right sides together. Slice diagonally from corner to corner to create 354 matched triangle pairs. Sew triangle pairs with ¼″ seam to yield 354 half square triangle units. Press seams to the black fabric and snip dog ears. Units should measure 2″ unfinished, 1 ½″ finished.

Slice the remaining 354 black squares from corner to corner on the diagonal to yield 708 wing triangles.

E

Stitch a wing triangle to either side of the 354 half-square triangle units as shown, pressing seams to the black triangles just added. Clip dog ears.

Wing Triangle Border Unit

From the light/neutral scraps, cut 50 – 3 ⅞″ squares. Slice squares once on the diagonal from corner to corner to yield 100 triangles.

F

Join these triangles to the pieced wing triangle unit. Press seams toward the neutral triangle. Trim dog ears. (Reserve the remaining 254 Wing Triangle Units for the sashing.)

Blue String Cornerstones

Following directions for string blocks on pages 6-9, prepare 72 – 3 ½″ paper foundation squares.

G

Add strips to either side of the center strip until the paper base is completely covered. Press. Square units to 3 ½″ and remove the paper. Make 72.

Red Strings

Prepare 64 – 5 ½″ foundation squares.

H

Add strips to either side of the center strip until the paper base is completely covered. Press. Square units to 5 ⅛″. Slice the blocks from corner to corner once on the diagonal across the strings to yield 128 string triangles. Carefully remove the paper.

String Sashing Unit

I

Stitch a reserved black Wing Triangle Unit to either side of a red Sashing Triangle to complete one string sashing unit. Press seams toward the black triangles. Clip dog ears. Make 127.

Layout

Referring to the Quilt Assembly Diagram on page 37, position the individual star blocks, red string sashing units and blue string cornerstones as shown, paying attention to the direction of the strings in the blue cornerstones. Please note that dark background stars alternate with light background stars in a checkerboard fashion. Stitch the quilt center into rows and join the rows to complete the quilt center.

Borders

Inner Border

Cut 8 – 2″ x width of fabric strips. Join the 8 border strips end to end with diagonal seams to make a strip approximately 320″ long. Trim excess ¼″ from seams and press seams open.

Lay the quilt center out on the floor, smoothing it gently. Do not tug or pull. Measure the quilt through the center from top to bottom. Cut two inner side borders this length. Sew the inner side borders to the quilt sides with right sides together, pinning to match centers and ends. Ease where necessary to fit. Press seams toward the borders.

Repeat for top and bottom inner borders, measuring across the quilt center, including the borders just added in the measurement. Cut top and bottom inner borders this length. Stitch the top and bottom inner borders to the quilt center, pinning to match centers and ends, easing where necessary to fit. Press seams toward borders.

Pieced Outer Border

Top and Bottom Spacer Units

From the black scraps cut 2 – 4 ¼″ squares.

From the neutral scraps cut 2 – 4 ¼″ squares.

Layer the black squares and light squares with right-sides together. Cut from corner to corner twice on the diagonal with an X to yield 8 matched pairs. Because the hour glass units are made with 4 different fabrics in each, you will have some extra pairs.

J

Choose which 4 pairs you want, and stitch into 4 half hour-glass units, pressing seams toward the black triangles. Join 2 pairs to create each hour-glass unit. Make 2 hour glass units.

Side Borders

Join 13 border units with the black triangles all pointing left. Make 2.

Join 13 Border units with the black triangles all pointing right. Make 2.

K

Referring to the diagram, join a left pointing border section to a right pointing border section. Make 2.

Sew the side borders to the quilt sides with right sides together, pinning to match centers and ends. Ease where necessary to fit. Press seams toward the inner borders.

Top and Bottom Borders

The Top and bottom borders are pieced the same way, with one fewer unit per end, and the 3″ hour glass units are in the center.

Join 12 Border units with the black triangles all pointing left. Make 2.

Join 12 Border units with the black triangles all pointing right. Make 2.

L

Referring to the diagram, join the left facing border half and the right facing border half with the hour glass unit in the center. Make 2.

Sew the top and bottom borders to the quilt sides with right sides together, pinning to match centers and ends. Ease where necessary to fit. Press seams toward the inner borders.

Finishing

Orca Bay is quilted in an antique beige thread, in an edge to edge design called Feather Meander #1 by Jessica Schick. Refer to the resources page for contact information. A simple solid black binding finishes the edge of the quilt.

Orca Bay
Directions At-A-Glance

A

HOURGLASS HALF UNIT
Make 448 half hour-glass units

B

HOURGLASS UNIT
Make 224 hour-glass units

C
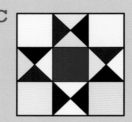
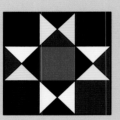

HOURGLASS BLOCKS
Make 28 each

D
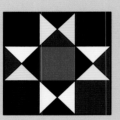

HALF-SQUARE TRIANGLE UNIT
2″ unfinished
Make 354

E

WING UNITS
Make 354

F

WING TRIANGLE BORDER UNIT
Make 100

G

BLUE STRING CORNERSTONE
3 ½″ unfinished
Make 72

H

RED STRING SASHING TRIANGLES
5 1/8″ unfinished string square
Cut in half across the strings to make
128 triangles

I

STRING SASHING UNIT
Make 127

J

**BORDER
SPACER
UNIT**
Make 2

K

SIDE BORDERS
Make 2

L

TOP AND BOTTOM BORDERS
Make 2

**ASSEMBLY
DIAGRAM**

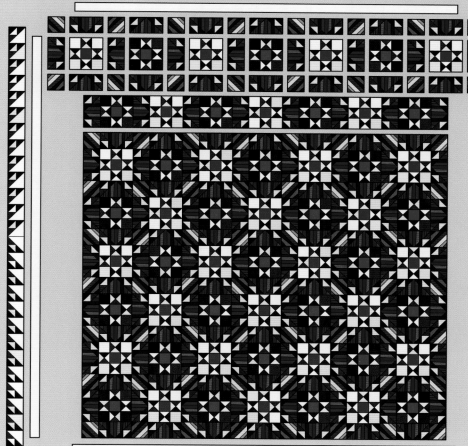

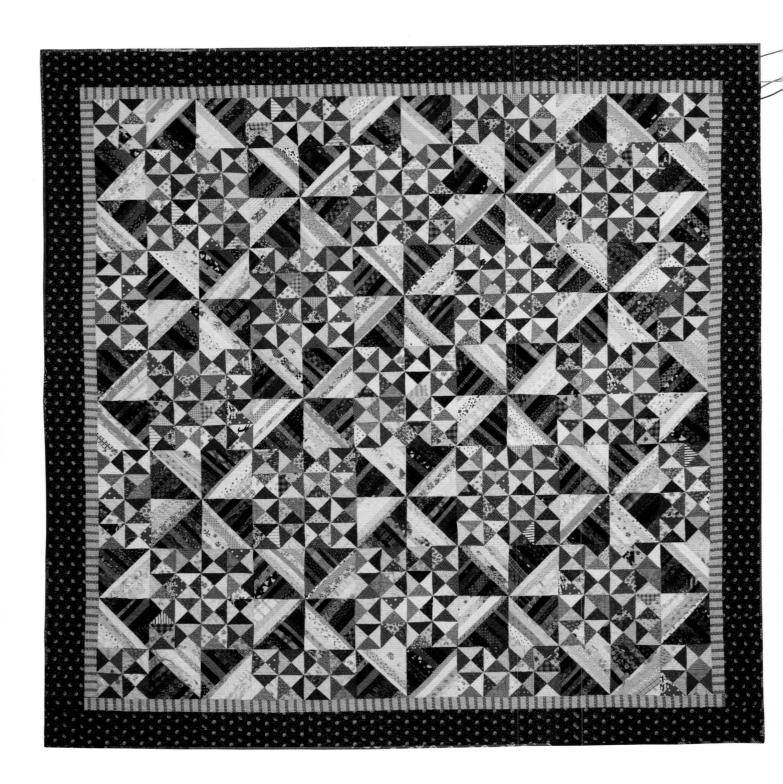

Pfeffernüsse

QUILT SIZE: 84 ½″ SQUARE

BLOCK SIZE: 12″

A trip to Germany in February of 2011 sparked a love of my family heritage on my mother's side of the family. As we drove through the winter countryside, I was filled with a longing for family members long past, that I had never gotten to know. Did they travel these same areas? Did they cook Pfeffernüsse (pepper-nut) cookies at holiday time? I'll never know, but I like to dream they did! The warm browns and reds in this quilt bring to mind the delicious smells of spice cookies baking in my oven. See the end of the pattern for the recipe!

Fabric Requirements

3 yards of brown scraps and strings in a wide variety of spicy brown hues from light to dark for string blocks

4 yards of neutral/light scraps and strings in a wide variety of shades of white to cream to beige for hour glass and string blocks.

Note: All of these fabrics can have other colors playing on them. There may be red hearts on a white background, but it will still read as neutral/light. There may be green leaves and pink flowers on a cream background, but it will still read as light. Don't think that these have to be tone-on-tone! Look at the background color of the fabric and let it play!

2 ½ yards of red scraps for the hourglass blocks

½ yard tan stripe for the inner border

1 ¼ yard brown stripe for the outer border

String Units

Following the directions for string blocks on pages 6-9, prepare 72 – 7 ½″ foundation squares.

Neutral Units

For the neutral units only it is helpful to start with a 2″ strip down the center diagonal of your foundation since we will be sub-cutting these units down the center diagonal. Continue adding strips until the entire foundation is covered. Trim to 7 ½″ square. Make 36.

Diagrams are on page 42-43.

A

Referring to the diagram, slice the units from corner to corner through the center strip and remove the paper. Make 72 triangles.

Brown Triangles

Start covering the foundations by laying two strips right sides together across the center diagonal of the foundation square. Continue adding strips until the entire foundation is covered. Trim to 7 ½″ square. Make 36.

B

Referring to the diagram, slice the units from corner to corner across the strings and remove the paper. Make 72 triangles.

C

To complete the unit, sew a brown triangle to a neutral triangle with right-sides together and stitch. Press toward the neutral. Repeat for all 72 pairs. Press toward the neutral and trim to 6 ½″ square.

Hour-Glass Units

I used the Companion Angle Ruler and 2″ strips from my scraps to cut the quarter-square triangles used for this quilt. The traditional method of using 4 ¼″ squares is given for those who do not have access to this ruler. Please see section on Using Specialty Rulers found on pages 94-95. You can use any method that gives you a 3 ½″ unfinished hour-glass unit that finishes at 3″.

From the red scraps cut 144 – 4 ¼″ squares.

From the neutral scraps cut 144 – 4 ¼″ squares.

Layer the dark squares and light squares with right sides together. Cut from corner to corner twice on the diagonal with an X to yield 576 matched pairs.

D

Stitch into 576 half hourglass units, pressing seams toward the red triangles. Join two pairs to create each hour-glass unit. Make 288 hour glass units.

E

Join 4 hourglass units as shown to create 1 block quarter. Make 72. Each Pfefferneuse block uses two of these triangle units, and two string blocks.

F

Following string block placement as shown, combine triangle units and string units to complete 36 blocks as shown.

Quilt Assembly

Referring to the Quilt Assembly Diagram on page 43, lay out the blocks in 6 rows with 6 blocks each, rotating blocks to complete the design. Stitch the quilt center into rows. Join the rows to complete the quilt center.

Borders

Inner Border

Cut 8 – 2″ strips across the width of the fabric from selvage to selvage. Join the 8 border strips end to end with diagonal seams to make a strip approximately 320″ long. Trim excess ¼″ from seams and press seams open.

Lay the quilt center out on the floor, smoothing it gently. Do not tug or pull. Measure the quilt through the center from top to bottom. Cut two inner side borders this length. Sew the inner side borders to the quilt sides with right sides together, pinning to match centers and ends. Ease where necessary to fit. Press seams toward the borders.

Repeat for top and bottom inner borders, measuring across the quilt center, including the borders just added in the measurement. Cut top and bottom inner borders this length. Stitch the top and bottom inner borders to the quilt center, pinning to match centers and ends, easing where necessary to fit. Press seams toward borders.

Outer Border

From brown stripe, cut 8 – 5″ strips across the width of the fabric from selvage to selvage. Join the 8 border strips end to end on the straight of grain to make a strip approximately 320″ long. Press seams open. Add the outer borders in the same manner as the inner borders were added.

Finishing

Pfeffernüsse was machine quilted in antique gold thread with an edge to edge design called Damask Feathers by Hermoine Agee of Lorien Quilting, Australia. Refer to the resources page for contact information. A scrappy red binding was a great way to use up the left over reds from the hour-glass blocks!

Pfefferneuse Cookie Recipe

Ingredients

1 cup dark corn syrup

½ cup honey

2 cups white sugar

1 cup butter

1 egg

½ cup buttermilk

7 cups all-purpose flour

1 ¼ teaspoons salt

1 ½ teaspoons ground allspice

1 ½ teaspoons ground cinnamon

½ teaspoon ground cloves

1 ½ teaspoons baking soda

Directions

1. In a large bowl, cream together the margarine and sugar. Add corn syrup, egg and honey; mix well. Sift together the flour, salt, cinnamon, allspice, cloves, and baking soda; stir into the sugar mixture alternately with the buttermilk. Knead dough, which should be very stiff, by hand for 15 to 30 minutes. Divide dough into 2 pieces, flatten slightly, wrap in plastic, and refrigerate 3 hours or overnight.

2. Preheat oven to 350 degrees F (175 degrees C). Roll out dough to ¼ inch thickness and cut into 1 inch squares. Place on an un-greased cookie sheet and bake for 15 to 25 minutes, testing to see if they are done.

When cool, roll them in powered sugar and keep them in an airtight container.

Pfefferneuse
Directions At-A-Glance

A
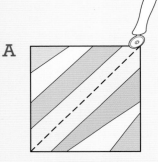

NEUTRAL STRING UNIT
7 ½″ unfinished
Make 36

B

BROWN STRING UNIT
7 ½″ unfinished
Make 36

C
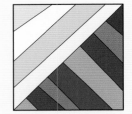

COMPLETED STRING UNIT
6 ½″ unfinished
Make 72

D

HOURGLASS UNIT
3 ½″ unfinished
Make 288

E
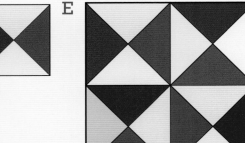

HOURGLASS 4 PATCH
6 ½″ unfinished
Make 72

F

PFEFFERNEUSEBLOCK
12 ½″ unfinished
Make 36

ASSEMBLY DIAGRAM

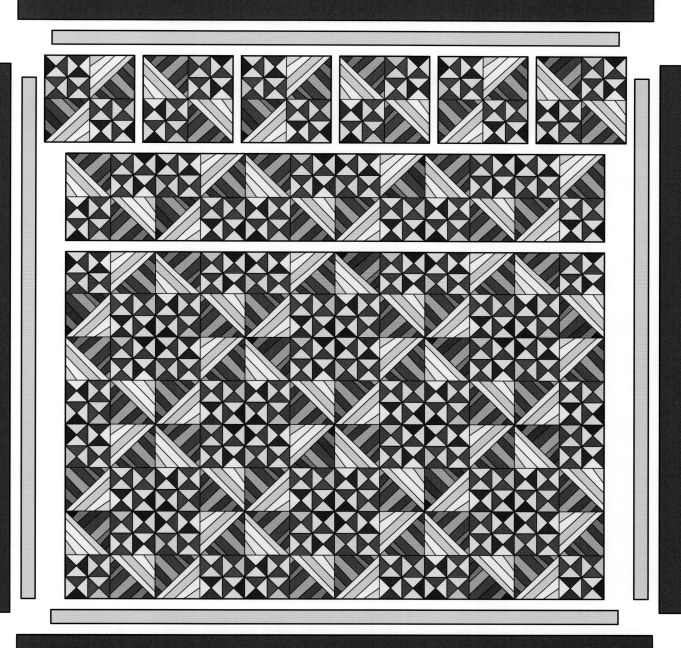

44

Pineapple Crazy

QUILT SIZE: 80˝ x 90˝

BLOCK SIZE: 5˝

You know you are scrap-crazy when you have to STOP the vacuum from sucking up a small 2˝ triangle because it just might be the perfect piece for "somewhere." If you have been saving every string, scrap and crumb, this quilt is the "somewhere" for you! At least once in our lifetime, every quilter desires to do one Extreme Quilt. This was definitely one that was on my bucket list – and I enjoyed every scrappy moment of it! Number of pieces in my quilt? 12,000!

Fabric Requirements

5 yards assorted colored scraps and strings – clean out the small saved bits, and let's use them!

5 yards assorted neutral/light scraps and strings – I've got everything from old calicoes to novelties with baseballs and everything in between.

2 yards solid red – enough for block and border accents and binding.

All the blocks in this quilt – the pineapple blocks, border triangle blocks, and the corner blocks – use foundation paper piecing in construction. All of the blocks finish at 5˝ making the quilt very easy to assemble.

You will find the templates for each unit on pages 50-51.

Copy the required number of templates onto printer paper, tracing paper, tissue or foundation of your choice. I do not recommend vellum paper as it curls and shrinks when ironing. Due to the many, many seams in this quilt, and the number of seam allowances adding bulk, I do not recommend piecing these on a fabric foundation, making things even bulkier. I prefer to use paper, and remove it before quilt assembly.

Pineapple Blocks

Diagrams are on page 48-49.

A

Make 224 paper foundations for pineapple blocks.

The first thing to notice is that this block is not colored the same as a traditional pineapple. It has 3 light corners and one dark. This is reflected on the paper foundation template on page 50.

Piece all blocks and trim to 5 ½˝ square unfinished. Remove all papers.

B

Join blocks into groups of 4 as shown, bringing dark corners together and stitch. Make 56 – 4-block units. This block unit should measure 10 ½˝ square unfinished and 10˝ finished

Border Blocks

C

Make 60 paper foundations for the border blocks.

Piece all blocks following paper piecing directions on page 46.

Paper Piecing Basics

Some things to remember about foundation piecing: Keep stitches small. A 1.5 setting is ideal.

Begin by centering fabric #1 behind area #1 on the foundation, placing the wrong side of the fabric against the unprinted side of the foundation. Look through the foundation, and position it so there is at least ¼″ of seam allowance extending beyond the line separating area #1 from area #2. A small dot of glue stick can hold piece #1 in place – pins can distort the paper.

Place piece #2 against piece #1 with right sides together, extending seam allowance beyond the piecing line. Cutting pieces larger than needed will make positioning easier.

As you add fabrics to the block for each step, place them in the correct position on the unprinted side of the foundation as noted by the numbers on the pattern. It helps to place them where they will be in the finished position after they have been sewn – keeping the cut edges together along the seam line, flip the piece you are adding so that it is right sides together to the piece you are adding it to.

Holding the block up toward a window or other light source can help with piece placement. Sew all seams by stitching directly on the line on the printed side of the foundation, extending the seam line a few stitches into the seam allowance at either end of the seam. Future seam lines will cross these and lock them in place. Back tacking is not necessary.

Press each seam after it has been sewn. Use a dry, warm iron, making sure that each seam is pressed completely to the side. Any tucks or pleats you create during pressing will affect the accuracy of the points or corners within your block.

Trim each seam as each piece is added. Because these blocks are so small, I trimmed a bit smaller than the traditional ¼″ seam, but kept the seams more than ⅛″. I tend to trim with scissors, rather than taking the time to lay everything back on a mat with a ruler and rotary cutter.

If while sewing, you find yourself with a torn foundation, grab some printer mailing labels, cut them into narrow strips and use those as "paper band-aids" to hold your foundations back together. These won't melt when being touched with the iron, as regular tape will.

After piecing, trim each unit by placing the ¼″ line of a ruler on the seam line of the block, trimming each unit ¼″ beyond the seam line. At this point, before assembling the quilt, remove all the paper.

Position and add the first neutral strip to the border block by stitching on the line. Trim seam and press. Repeat for opposite side of the border block triangle. Trim seam and press. Now turn the block over, and working from the front of the block, continue to add strings, strips and scraps until the foundation is filled. Most of my border blocks have at least 3 strings on either side of the center pieced triangle, but may have as many as 4 or 5.

Trim blocks and remove paper. Units will measure 5 ½″ square unfinished and 5″ finished.

Corner Blocks

D

Prepare 16 foundations for the corner units.

These units are small, finishing at only 2″ square, and paper piecing was a great way to use up the left over red from the centers of my pineapples and border triangles.

Following color placement, piece all 16 corner units using solid red and a variety of neutrals. Trim blocks and remove paper. Units will measure 2 ½″ square unfinished, 2″ finished.

Connectors

From neutral scraps cut 16 – 1 ½″ squares

From colored scraps cut 16 – 1 ½″ squares

From solid red cut 4 – 1 ½″ red squares.

E

Join each neutral square to a colored square. Press toward the colored square.

Corner Block Assembly

F

Lay out 4 corner units, 4 connectors and one red center square as shown.

Stitch the units into rows, and join rows to complete corner block. Make 4 corner blocks.

Quilt Assembly

Lay out pineapple units with 7 across and 8 down. Stitch quilt center into rows and join rows to complete quilt center.

Borders

G

Side Borders

Join 16 Border units side by side to create 1 side border. Repeat for second side border. Sew the side borders to the quilt sides with right sides together, pinning to match centers and ends. Press seams toward the borders.

Top and Bottom Borders

Join 14 border units side by side as shown for each top and bottom border. Add a corner block to each end of both borders, pressing seam toward the border. Sew the top and bottom borders to the quilt with right sides together, pinning to match centers and ends. Press seams toward the borders.

Finishing

Pineapple Crazy is machine quilted in an antique gold thread with an edge to edge design called Radiance by Urban Elementz. Refer to the resources page for contact information. A solid red binding ties all the other red accents in the quilt together.

Pineapple Crazy
Directions At-A-Glance

A

PINEAPPLE BLOCK
5 ½″ unfinished
Make 224

B

PINEAPPLE BLOCK UNIT
10 ½″ unfinished • Make 56

C

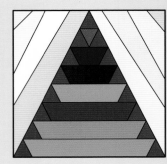

BORDER UNITS
5 ½″ unfinished
Make 60

D

CORNER UNIT
2 ½″ unfinished
Make 16

E

CONNECTOR UNIT
1 ½″ x 2 ½″ unfinished
Make 16

F

CORNER BLOCK
5 ½″ unfinished
Make 4

G

BORDERS
Make 2 side borders with 16 Border blocks each as shown on the top diagram.

Make top and bottom borders with 14 Border blocks each and 2 Corner blocks on each end.

48

ASSEMBLY DIAGRAM

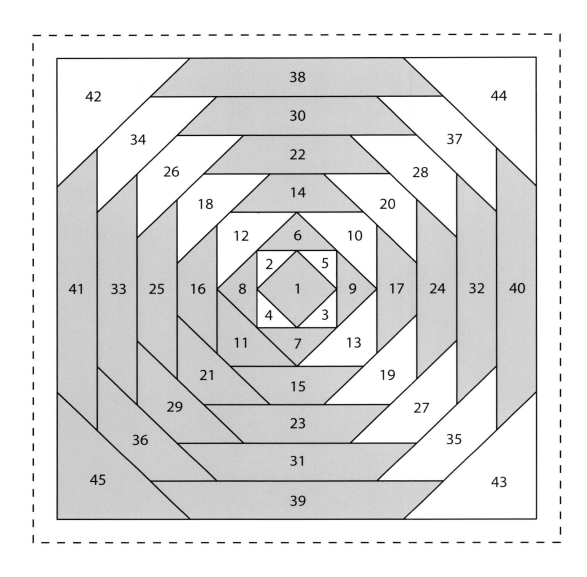

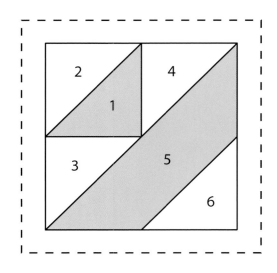

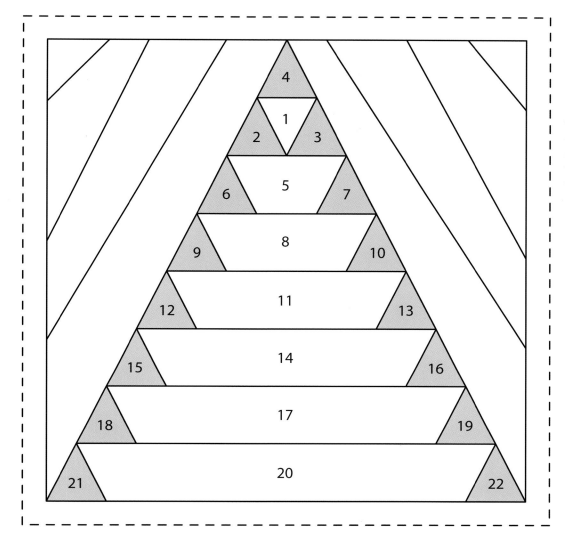

The lines on each side of the triangle are placement suggestions. You can use these or make up your own lines.

Roll Roll, Cotton Boll

QUILT SIZE: APPROX 85˝ x 100˝

One October morning my hubby Dave and I were driving from Smithfield, Va. back to our home in Wallburg, N.C., just outside of Winston Salem. We happened to be stuck on an impassable stretch of country road, following a truck just packed with cotton bales. I watched stray fluffs of raw cotton dropping and rolling off the back of that truck for miles – finding their place to land at the side of the road, leaving a path of cotton trailing behind. These blocks with their directional triangles remind me of the motion of those cotton bolls – watch them roll!

Fabric Requirements

5 yards of light/neutral scraps and strings. Look for a wide variety of prints, stripes, plaids and novelties ranging from white to cream to beige to tan. May include small figures, leaves and flowers as long as the fabric ground reads as neutral.

1 ¾ yards of red print for blocks

2 yards of pink scraps for block centers and pieced border

1 ½ yards of brown scraps for blocks and pieced border

1 ½ yards of green scraps for blocks and pieced border

½ yard of green for inner border

Cotton Boll Blocks

I made each of the 30 block centers from different fabrics with no two blocks the same. Even though some of the fabrics repeat in other blocks, they are mixed with other fabrics. Mix and match block parts as desired. One constant red is used in the triangle sashings around the block center to tie the blocks together. Directions are given to complete 1 block center. There are 30 Cotton Boll blocks in the quilt.

Block Centers

From the same red fabric used in the block sashing, cut 30 – 2˝ red squares to be used as block centers.

Diagrams are on pages 57-59.

Large Half-Square Triangles

I used the Easy Angle Ruler and 3 ½˝ strips from my scraps to cut the triangles used for this section. The traditional method of using 3 ⅞˝ squares is given for those who do not have access to this ruler. Please see section on Using Specialty Rulers found on pages 94-95. You can use any method that gives you a 3 ½˝ unfinished half-square triangle unit that finishes at 3˝.

From brown cut: 2 matching 3 ⅞˝ squares.

From pink cut: 2 matching 3 ⅞˝ squares.

A

Lay the brown squares and the pink squares with right sides together. Slice diagonally from corner to corner to create 4 matched triangle pairs. Sew triangle pairs with ¼˝ seam to yield 4 half-square triangle units. Press seams to the brown fabric and snip dog ears. Units should measure 3 ½˝ and finish at 3˝.

Spacer Units

B

Stitch a 2˝ x 8 ½˝ green rectangle to a 2˝ x 8 ½˝ neutral rectangle along the long side of the rectangle. Press seams toward the green, and sub-cut into 4 units as shown. There is ½˝ excess included for trimming.

From the same green, cut 4 - 2˝ corner squares.

C

Arrange the 4 matching triangle units with the spacers as shown, adding in a red 2″ square as the center. Sew block units into rows, and join rows to complete the block.

D

Referring to the diagram, frame the block with 4 sashing units, paying close attention to the direction that the sashing is turned. Add the 4 green squares that match the spacer units as block corners. Stitch the units into rows, and join rows to complete the block. Make 30.

Triangle Sashing

I used the Easy Angle Ruler and 2″ strips from my red and neutral fabrics to cut the triangles used for this section. The traditional method of using 2 ³/₈″ squares is given for those who do not have access to this ruler. You can use any method that gives you a 2″ unfinished half-square triangle unit that finishes at 1 ½″.

Small half-square triangles

From the light/neutral fabrics cut: 300 – 2 ³/₈″ squares.

From the red print cut: 300 – 2 ³/₈″ squares.

Lay red squares and neutral squares with right sides together. Slice diagonally from corner to corner to make 600 matched triangle pairs. Sew triangle pairs with ¼″ seam to yield 600 half-square triangle units. Press seams to the red fabric and snip dog ears. Units should measure 2″ unfinished and 1 ½″ finished.

E

Following the diagram, stitch 5 triangles side by side to create 1 block sashing unit. Make 120.

Alternate String blocks

Following the directions for string blocks on pages 6-9, prepare 60 – 8 ½″ foundation squares.

F

Add strips to either side of the center strip until the foundation is completely covered. Press as you sew. Square units to 8 ½″. Slice the units on the diagonal from corner to corner across the strings and remove the paper. Make 120 triangle units.

Reserve 4 of the string pieced triangle units for the corners.

G

Stitch the remaining 116 string triangles into string block halves as shown. You will have 58 of these 2-string triangle units.

H

Set aside 18 of these units, and stitch the remaining 40 into alternate setting blocks as shown.

Trim string blocks to 11″ unfinished, 10 ½″ finished.

Quilt Center Assembly

Roll Roll, Cotton Boll is an "on-point" setting, and assembled in diagonal rows. I specifically designed it this way for ease of construction so there would not be bias on the outside edges of the blocks when they were sewn together.

Referring to the Quilt Assembly Diagram on page 59, lay out the blocks and setting squares, filling in the sides with the setting triangles and corners. I like to piece diagonally set quilts into two halves. This keeps things from being too unwieldy, especially when sewing a large quilt top. Join quilt top halves to complete quilt center. Press.

Trimming

Trim the quilt center, leaving ¼″ seam allowance beyond the green corner squares in each block, around the outside edge of the top. Stay stitch around the edge by setting the machine at a large stitch length and stitching just inside of that ¼″ measurement. This will help keep the strings from coming unstitched, and add some stability to the edge of the quilt center.

Borders

Inner Border

From the green fabric, cut 9 – 1 ¾″ strips x the width of fabric.

Join the strips end to end with diagonal seams to create one long length, measuring approximately 360″. Trim the excess ¼″ beyond seams. Press the seams open.

Lay quilt out on the floor, smoothing it gently. Do not tug or pull. Measure the quilt through the center from top to bottom and cut two inner side borders this length. Sew the inner side borders to the quilt sides with right sides together, pinning to match centers and ends. Ease where necessary to fit. Press seams to the borders.

Repeat steps for top and bottom inner borders, measuring across the width of the quilt including the borders just added. Cut top and bottom inner borders this length. Sew to quilt top and bottom with right sides together, pinning to match centers and ends. Ease where necessary to fit. Press seams to the borders.

Outer Pieced Border

Join two 2″ pink strips on either side of a green 2″ strip, to make one panel, pressing seams toward the green center strip. Cut 2″ sub-cuts from the panel. Make as many scrappy panels as you needed from different pinks and greens to give you 166 sub-cuts. If strips are full width of fabric yardage, you can get 16 per strip set. If strips are long, think about cutting the lengths in half and mixing and matching up the sets for more variety. Adjust as necessary depending upon your strip lengths. What is important is doing what you need to do to get the number of sub-cuts needed.

Setting triangles

I used my Companion Angle ruler and 1 ½″ strips for the quarter square setting triangles for this border. The traditional method of cutting squares is given for those who don't have access to this ruler.

From brown scraps cut 83 – 3 ¼″ squares. Slice these squares corner to corner on the diagonal twice with an X to give you the 332 quarter square triangles needed.

I

Following the diagram, stitch a brown triangle to either end of each border section as shown. Press seam toward the brown triangles. Make 166.

J

Side Borders: Join 39 border units side by side as shown. Press.

Top and Bottom Borders: Join 32 border units side by side as shown. Press. There should be 24 left over parallelograms to be used in the next step.

Border Ends and Corners

K

Each border end and corner uses 2 of the left over border parallelograms. Un-stitch one brown triangle from the top of one parallelogram and save it for the far right end of the unit. Un-stitch the second parallelogram between the center green square and the pink square above it.

Re-arrange as shown and join these units to create 1 border end and corner. Make 12.

Left Border Ends

L

Stitch a border end to the left side of each of the side, top and bottom borders, turning the border into a trapezoidal shape.

Join the side borders to the quilt center, pinning to match centers and extending ends ¼″ beyond the edge of the quilt center – these are the dog ears! Ease where necessary to fit. Press seams toward the inner border.

Add the top and bottom borders to the quilt in the same way, pinning to match centers and ends, extending the ends ¼″ beyond the edge of the center and overlapping the ends of the side borders – easing where necessary to fit. Press seams toward the inner border.

Border Corners

M

For each corner of the quilt, join two border corners as shown into one corner unit. Make 4.

Sew a corner unit to each corner of the quilt to complete the pieced border surrounding the quilt. There should be ¼″ depth of seam allowance at each corner of the quilt to prevent the loss of the corner of the green inner border within in the seam.

Finishing

Roll Roll, Cotton Boll is quilted in a tan thread in an edge-to-edge design called Twirly Feathers by Hermione Agee of Lorien Quilting, Australia. Refer to the resources page for contact information. The quilt is bound in a brown print.

A

LARGE HALF-SQUARE TRIANGLE UNIT
3 ½˝ unfinished
Make 4 per block
120 total

B

SPACER UNITS
2˝ x 3 ½˝ unfinished
Make 4 per block
120 total

C

BLOCK CENTER
8˝ unfinished
Make 30

D

ROLL ROLL, COTTON BOLL BLOCK
11˝ unfinished
Make 30

E

TRIANGLE SASHING
Make 120

F

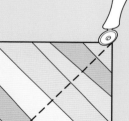
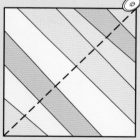

ALTERNATE BLOCK FOUNDATION
8 ½˝ unfinished
Make 60
Cut in half on the diagonal across the strings to make 120 triangles.

G

ALTERNATE BLOCK SETTING TRIANGLES
Make 58

H

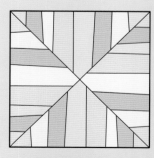

ALTERNATE BLOCKS
11˝ unfinished
Make 40

I

OUTER BORDER UNITS
Make 166

J

OUTER BORDER
To make 2 side borders, join 39 units each. To make the top and bottom borders, join 32 units each.

K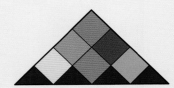

BORDER ENDS AND CORNERS
Make 12

L

LEFT BORDER ENDS
Make 4

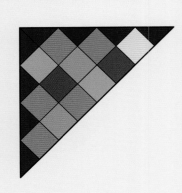 

M

BORDER CORNERS
Make 4

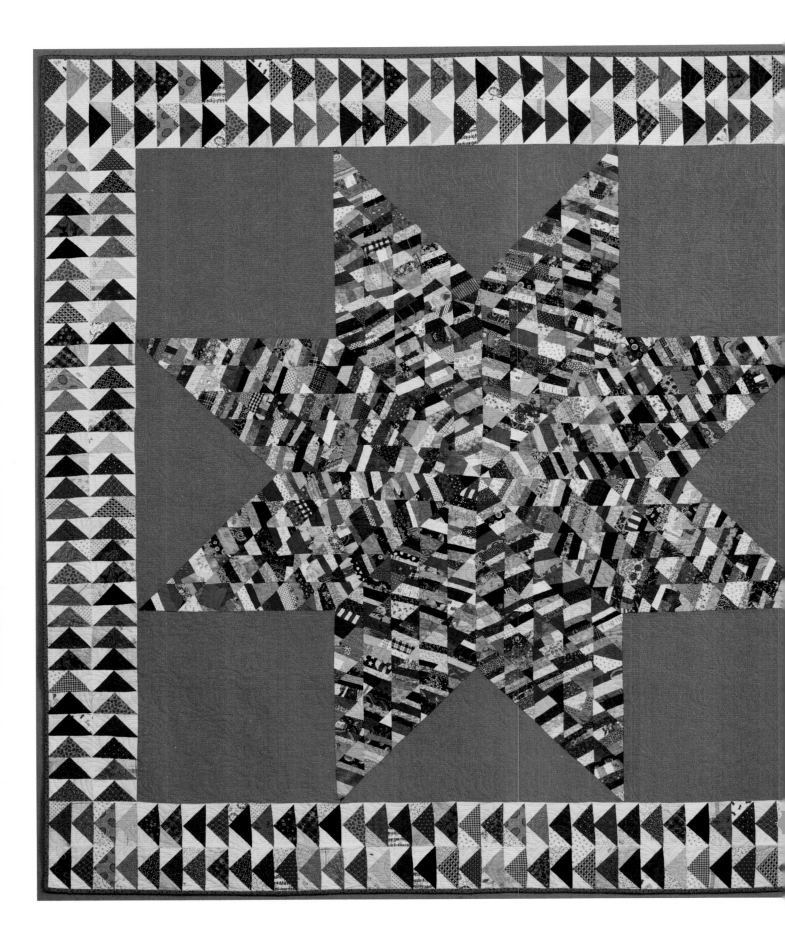

Santa Fe String Star

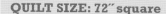

QUILT SIZE: 72˝ square

My love of antique string quilts prodded me into making this reproduction of a beloved 8-pointed string star. Hot-hot orange is the perfect background for a quilt with loads of vibrant color and a wide variety of scraps – some dating as far back as the 1950s! The double flying geese border, with its light background triangles, counterbalance all the colors in the quilt center bringing daylight to the outside of the quilt. A turquoise binding brings color to the edge!

Fabric Requirements

1 ¾ yards of orange tone-on-tone for the background

4 yards of colored scraps and strings for the center star and flying geese border

1 ¾ yards of neutral/light scraps for the flying geese border

Additional Requirements

Chalk pencil

Template plastic

Star Points

Trace the diamond shaped template found on page 64 onto the template plastic and cut out. *Note:* the template includes seam allowance.

Trace and cut 200 diamond foundations. Be accurate when tracing and cutting.

Diagrams are on page 65-66.

A

Start with a strip down the center of each diamond. Add strips to either side of the center strip until the foundation is completely covered. Press as you sew. Trim to paper shape and remove the foundation paper. Diamonds should measure 4˝ per side, and will finish at 3 ¼˝ per side.

Make 200.

Star Point Assembly

B

Each of the eight assembled star points has 25 diamonds stitched into 5 rows of 5 diamonds each. Sew the diamonds side-by-side as shown. Press seams all in one direction. Make 40

Join 5 of the diamond rows together, pinning to match intersections. Press seams all in one direction. Make 8 large diamond sections.

Quilt Top Center Assembly

From orange fabric cut:

4 – 16 ⅞˝ squares for the corner blocks

1 – 24 ½˝ square, cut from corner to corner with an X to yield 4 side triangles

Sewing those Y-seams!

It's not as hard as it looks. The single simple thing that you need to remember is to not sew into your seam allowances.

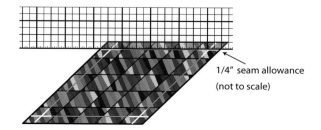

1/4˝ seam allowance (not to scale)

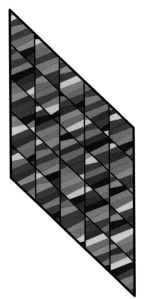

Use a ruler with a good ¼″ marking and a chalk pencil to mark your seam allowances where seam lines will cross. Marking the whole seam isn't necessary, but you need to know where seams will meet to avoid sewing into the seam allowance. Mark the seam crossing on all corners of the large diamonds, and one corner of each corner setting square, as well as the bottom corner of each setting side triangle.

Place two of the large pieced diamonds right sides together, and stitch the ¼″ seam, back-tacking to begin and end each seam, but keeping stitches OUT of the seam allowance area.

Referring to the Quilt Assembly Diagram on page 67, join two quarters into halves, remembering to keep stitching out of the seam allowances, and using the above technique, set in one side triangle. Repeat with remaining star point sections, forming a second star half.

Stitch Star halves together, remembering to keep stitching out of the seam allowance. Inset remaining two side triangles to quilt center. Press and trim seam allowances.

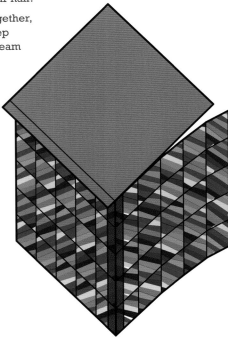

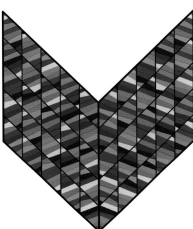

Press this seam open and trim the dog ears.

Borders

This border is meant to fit a star center that measures 56 ½″ square unfinished. Measure your star. You may have to adjust your borders if it is bigger or smaller than 56″.

Flying Geese Units

I used both my Companion Angle ruler and Easy Angle ruler to cut the pieces I needed for the geese from my stash of 2 ½″ scrap strips. If you don't have the rulers or an abundance of 2 ½″ strips handy, you might like this speedy method that makes 2 flying geese units at one time.

Start with a 5 ¼″ square of geese fabric and 4 – 2 ⅞″ squares of neutral/light.

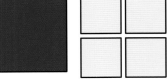

Position a corner square with right sides together against a diamond as shown, and sew, back stitching where the square meets the seam of the two diamonds, and complete the seam all the way to the edge of the square. Back tack and remove from machine.

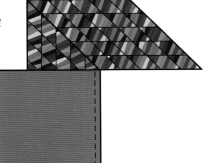

Reposition the unit to sew the remaining seam starting at the point where the 3 seams meet and keeping stitches away from the seam allowance. It is better to be one stitch short of the seam, than to cross it with even one stitch. Stitch all the way to the end. Press and trim dog ears. Repeat to make 4 units.

Lay two of the 2 ⅞″ squares on top of the 5 ¼″ geese square with right sides together, lining them up with the top left and lower right corners overlapping them in the center. Draw a diagonal line through the smaller squares. Sew a scant ¼″ on each side of the marked diagonal. Cut apart on the marked diagonal.

Press the seams away from the geese triangles. Place another small, neutral square in the corner of the geese triangle, with right sides together. Draw a diagonal line on the back of the neutral square. Sew a scant ¼″ on each side of the marked line. Cut apart on the marked line. Repeat with the remaining 2 pieces to yield 2 flying geese units.

C
Make 256 flying geese units.

D
Stitch 2 geese units side by side in pairs.

Side borders

E
Join 28 geese pairs together to form each of the 2 side border as shown. Join 36 geese pairs together to form each of the top/bottom borders as shown.

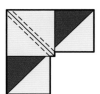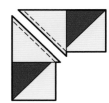

Refer to Quilt Assembly Diagram on page 67 to see the way the geese fly! They go up the left side, to the right across the top, down the right side and to the left on the bottom.

Sew the side borders to the quilt sides with right sides together, pinning to match centers and ends. Ease where necessary to fit. Press seams toward the borders.

Stitch the top and bottom borders to the quilt center, pinning to match centers and ends, easing where necessary to fit. Press seams toward borders.

Finishing

Santa Fe String Star is quilted in gold thread with an edge-to-edge design called Storm Watch by quiltersniche.com. Refer to the resources page for contact information. A teal blue binding adds just a touch of color, keeping the geese flying in formation around the quilt!

Star Point Template

Seam allowance included.
Make 200

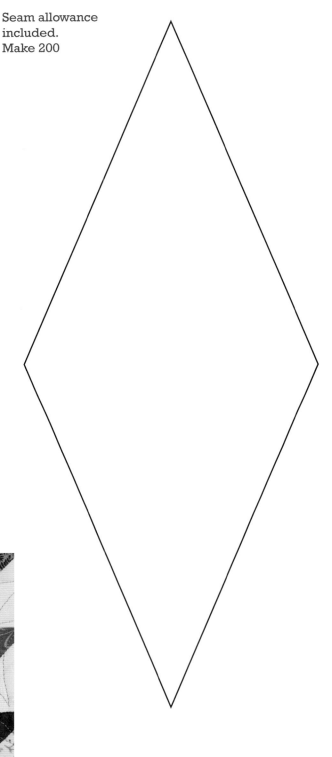

Santa Fe String Star
Directions At-A-Glance

A

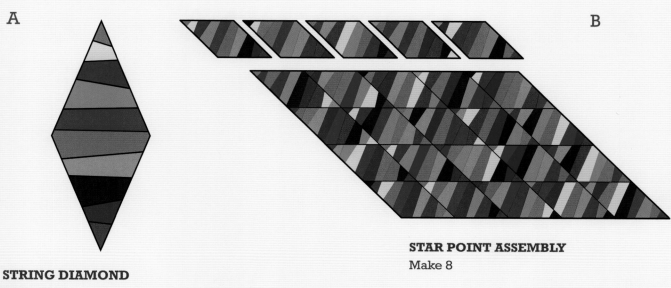

STRING DIAMOND
Make 200

STAR POINT ASSEMBLY
Make 8

B

C

FLYING GEESE UNIT
2 ½″ x 4 ½″ unfinished
Make 256

D

FLYING GEESE PAIRS
Make 128 units

E

BORDERS
Make 2 side borders with 28 pairs.
Make top and bottom with 36 pairs

This diagram does not match the photo of the quilt on page 60. The quilt was patterned so the outer border fits a 56 ½″ center. My quilt is slightly larger.

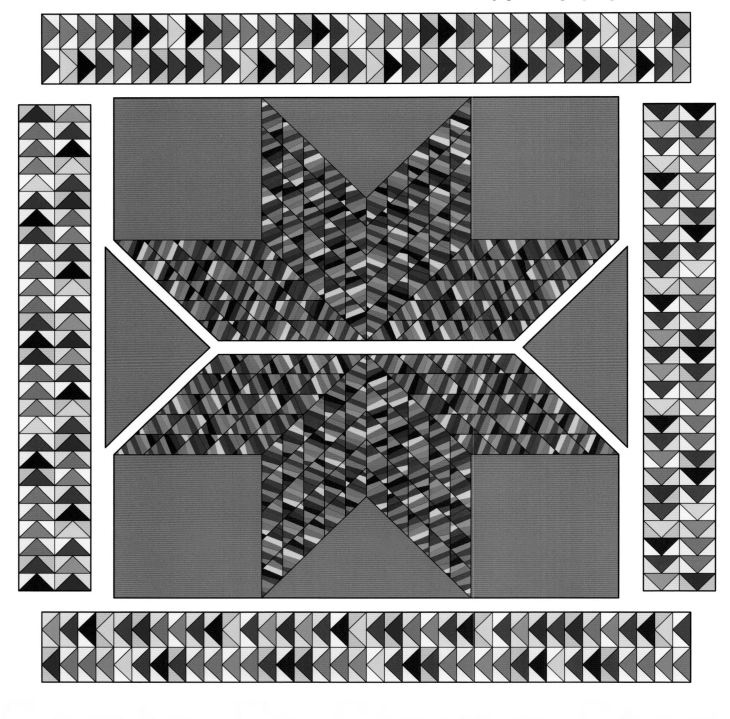

Talkin' Turkey!

QUILT SIZE: 84″ x 97 ½″

BLOCK SIZE: 12″ FINISHED

I **love** red! I am drawn to red fabric at every turn, especially when found in antique quilts. If I'm browsing for fabric, without anything particular in mind, I gravitate toward red. When I spent time digging through my strings, I found I had more red strings than **any** other color – even when compared to blue!

This presented a challenge – how far could I go with just these strings and scraps in **every** shade of red I could find- from pinky rosy red to orange rusty red to juicy tomato, fire engine and all the way to burgundy and everywhere in between? This is the result. I used **every** kind of fabric in here as long as it was red. You'll find funky Maryland crabs, Lucky Cows, Christmas fabrics, and even a gifted piece of Central Michigan Chippewas!

The neutral side is just as varied, including some "I dare ya" prints – as in "I dare ya to throw in those hideous Sun Bonnet Sues!" And I did. I even threw in some Millennium fabric. The more you throw in, and the more it clashes, the better it is. Believe me – though the design is based on a traditional Turkey Tracks block, this quilt is **no turkey**!

Fabric Requirements

5 yards of red scraps and strings

6 ½ yards of neutral/light scraps and strings

Red Strings Triangles

Following directions for string blocks on pages 6-9, prepare 60 – 5 ½″ paper foundation squares.

Diagrams are on page 72-73.

A

Start covering the foundations by laying two strips right sides together across the center diagonal of the foundation square. Sew the two pieces together, flip the top strip over and press. Continue adding strips until the entire foundation is covered. Trim to 5 ½″ and slice the blocks across the strings from corner to corner. Remove the paper. Make 120 triangles.

Center Nine-Patch Units

Note: These sections can be strip pieced, but as scraps and strips may vary in length, no number of strips to cut is given. What is important is that you sew enough strip sets to get the number of sub-cuts required. I pieced these with individual squares for more variety in placement.

From red scraps cut 150 – 2 ⅝″ squares

From neutral/light scraps cut 120 – 2 ⅝″ squares.

B

Sew a red square between two neutral squares to create 1 side unit. Press seam toward center red square. Make 60.

Sew 3 red squares side by side, and press seams away from the center square. Make 30.

Arrange the units as shown. Sew into nine-patch blocks. Blocks will be an odd size, measuring 6 ⅞″ square unfinished, 6 ⅜″ finished.

Adding String Triangles

C

Add 4 red string triangles to the four edges of each nine-patch. Press seams to the corners. They will be large, leaving a bit more than ¼″ seam allowance around the outside edge. Use a ruler with a ¼″ marked line to square the block down to size, leaving ¼″ seam allowance beyond each corner of the nine-patch. The blocks should measure 9 ½″ square unfinished and 9″ finished. Make 30.

Flying Geese Units

There is a whole flock of geese in this quilt! Each block has 8 flying geese units, for a total of 240. The border uses 216 more, bringing the total of geese in this quilt to 456! I used the Companion Angle ruler for my large geese triangles, and the Easy Angle Ruler for the side wing triangles, but you can use any method that gives you a geese triangle that finishes at 1 ½″ x 3″. The method below will give you two matching geese from each set of squares.

D1

Make 240 Flying Geese Units for the blocks.

For the blocks, cut:
60 - 4 ¼″ squares from the neutral/light scraps
240 - 2 3/8″ squares from the red scraps

Lay two of the red 2 ⅜″ squares on top of the 4 ¼″ neutral geese square with right sides together, lining them up with the top left and lower right corners overlapping them in the center. Draw a diagonal line through the smaller squares. Sew a scant ¼″ on each side of the marked diagonal. Cut apart on the marked diagonal.

Press the seams away from the geese triangles.

Place another small red square in the corner of the geese triangle, with right sides together. Draw a diagonal line on the back of the red square. Sew a scant ¼″ on each side of the marked line. Cut apart on the marked line. Repeat with the remaining two pieces to yield two flying geese units.

D2

Make 240 Flying Geese Units for the borders.

For the borders, cut: 54- 4 ½″ squares from the red scraps
216 - 2 ⅜″ squares from the neutral/light scraps. Repeat the process above to make the border units.

Neutral Bricks

2″ x 3 ½″ rectangles are used both in the blocks, and in the first border. We need 120 for the blocks and 66 for the border, bringing the total to 186.

E

From neutral light scraps cut 186 – 2″ x 3 ½″ rectangles. Reserve 66 for the border.

F

Using 240 of the geese units, and 120 of the neutral bricks – sew a brick between two geese units, and press seams toward the brick. Make 120, 4 per block.

Block Assembly

G

From light/neutral scraps cut 218 – 2″ squares. 120 are used for the blocks, 42 are cornerstones for the sashing and 56 are reserved for the borders.

H

Lay out the block center, surrounding it on 4 sides with the goose/rectangle units. Place 4 neutral 2″ squares in each corner. Assemble the block into rows and join rows to complete each block. Press seams toward the corner squares. Make 30.

Sashing and Cornerstones

The quilt is set with sashings that create a nine-patch where blocks join cornerstones.

From the neutral scraps cut 71 – 2″ x 9 ½″ rectangles.

From red scraps cut 162 – 2″ squares using 142 for the sashing. Reserve 20 for Border #1.

I

Sew a red square to the end of each sashing rectangle. Press seams toward the sashing.

Layout and Assembly

Referring to the Quilt Assembly Diagram on page 73, lay out the blocks in rows along with the sashings and cornerstones as shown. Stitch the quilt center into rows, pressing seams toward the sashing, and away from the cornerstones. Join the rows to complete the quilt center.

Borders

Border #1

This border doesn't look like a border at all! All it does is complete the nine patches along the edge of the quilt.

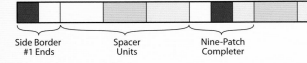

Side Border #1 Ends   Spacer Units   Nine-Patch Completer

Spacer unit

Sew 3 bricks side by side as shown. Press. Make 22.

Nine-patch completer

Sew a red 2″ square between two neutral 2″ squares. Press seams away from the red center square. Make 22.

Side Border #1 Ends

Sew a neutral 2″ square to a red 2″ square. Press seam toward the neutral square. Make 4

The diagram above shows 3 rectangle units alternated with 2 nine-patch completers.

Sew 5 – nine-patch completers (9P) alternating with 6 rectangle units (RU).

RU+9P+RU+9P+RU+9P+RU+9P+RU+9P+RU

Add a two square unit to Border #1 Ends as shown, ending the side Border #1's with a red square. Make 2.

Sew side Border #1s to quilt sides, pinning to match seams along the sides of the quilt. Press.

Top and Bottom border #1

Sew top and bottom borders by alternating 6 9Ps with 5 RUs

9P+RU+9P+RU+9P+RU+9P+RU+9P+RU+9P

Sew top and bottom border #1s to quilt sides, pinning to match seams along the sides of the quilt. Press.

Border #2 – Geese in a Row

Side #2 borders

From the reserved flying geese units, join 14 side by side to create 1 side border section. Make 4.

2 sections to either side of a 2″ neutral spacer square as shown. Press. Make 2.

Sew two side Border #2 to the quilt sides with neutral edge up against the quilt center. Press seams to one side.

Top and bottom #2 Borders

An additional 4 half-square triangle units are needed for the top and bottom borders. I used the Easy Angle ruler and 2″ scrap strips to make the half-square triangle units needed to complete the inner and outer geese border. The traditional method of using 2 ³⁄₈″ squares is given for those who do not have access to this ruler. Please see section on Using Specialty Rulers found on pages 94-95. You can use any method that gives you a 2″ unfinished half-square triangle unit that finishes at 1 ½″.

From red scraps cut 6 – 2 ³⁄₈″ squares.

From neutral scraps cut 6 – 2 ³⁄₈″ squares.

Layer the red squares and neutral squares with right sides together. Cut from corner to corner once on the diagonal to yield 12 matched pairs. Stitch into 12 half square triangle units, enough for completing the inner and outer goose borders. Press to the red triangle and remove dog ears.

Join 24 geese units side by side as for side borders. No spacer unit is required for the center of top and bottom borders. Add a half-square triangle to each end of top and bottom borders as shown on the quilt assembly diagram on page 75. Make 2. Attach the top and bottom Border #2 to the quilt with neutral triangles up against the quilt center. Press.

String Border #3

Cover approximately 16 – 8 ½″ x 11″ pieces of scrap paper with strings running down the length of the page from top to bottom. Short strings can be joined end to end to be long enough to lay the length of the paper. From each paper, cut 3 – 3 ½″ widths across the page from side to side. Recycled printer paper works great for this! Remove paper from all sections. Join the sections end to end to create one long string pieced border length of approximately 380 inches.

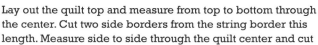

Lay out the quilt top and measure from top to bottom through the center. Cut two side borders from the string border this length. Measure side to side through the quilt center and cut a top and bottom border this length.

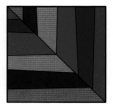

Faux Mitered Corners

I used my Easy Angle ruler and the left over length of string border to cut the triangles for the faux mitered corner blocks. Fold the length in half by bringing short ends together with right sides together and cut 4 triangle pairs using the 3 ½″ marking on the ruler.

If you do not have the Easy Angle Ruler, String piece 4 – 4″ blocks with the strings on the straight of the paper (Not diagonal). Square the edges. Remove the papers. Place the squares right sides together (with the strings going the same direction) and slice on the diagonal from corner to corner through both pairs.

Stitch the diagonal seam of each triangle pair. Trim to 3 ½″ square.

Add the side borders to the quilt center, pinning to match centers and ends. Press to the border. Add the faux mitered corner squares to each end of the top and bottom borders paying attention to which direction the strings fall. They should complete the border they are being added to. Stitch these to the quilt center, pinning to match centers and ends. Press to the inner red borders.

Border #4

Side borders

Following directions for goose borders in Border #2, join 15 geese side by side into 1 side border section. Make 4.

Sew 2 border sections to either side of 2″ neutral spacer squares. Press. Make 2. Add a half-square triangle unit to each end of the side border as shown.

Attach side borders to quilt, pinning to match centers and ends, and aligning each goose directly above the one on the other side of the string border from it. Stitch. Press.

Repeat the process for top and bottom outer borders, joining 26 geese units end to end. Add a half-square triangle unit as for the side borders to each end of the top and bottom border.

Add a 2″ neutral square to each end of the top and bottom borders. Press. Add top and bottom borders to quilt, pinning to match centers and ends, and pinning to align geese. Stitch. Press.

Finishing

Talkin' Turkey is quilted in a tan thread using an edge-to-edge design called Topiary Hearts by Urban Elementz. Refer to the resources page for contact information. A tan/beige stripe adds the perfect binding.

Talkin' Turkey!
Directions At-A-Glance

A

STRING TRIANGLES
60 – 5 ½″ string foundations
cut in half on the diagonal
Make 120

B

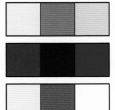

CENTER NINE-PATCH UNITS
Squares are cut 2 ⅝″
(150 red and 120 neutral)
Nine-Patch Units are
6 ⅞″ unfinished
Make 30

C

BLOCK CENTER
9 ½″ unfinished
Make 30

D1

BLOCKS FLYING
GEESE UNITS
2″ x 3 ½″ unfinished
Make 240

E

NEUTRAL BRICKS
2″ x 3 ½″ unfinished
Make 186 (reserve 66 for
the borders)

F

NEUTRAL BRICKS
2″ x 3 ½″ unfinished
Make 186 (reserve 66 for
the borders)

D2

**BORDERS FLYING
GEESE UNITS**
2″ x 3 ½″ unfinished
Make 216

G

**NEUTRAL SQUARES FOR
BLOCKS AND SASHING**
2″ unfinished
Make 218 (120 for blocks,
reserve 42 for sashing
cornerstones and 56 for
borders)

H

BLOCK ASSEMBLY
12 ½″ unfinished
Make 30

I

**SASHING AND
CORNERSTONE UNITS**
Cut 71 - 2″ x 9 ½″ neutral
rectangles
Cut 162 - 2″ red squares
(reserve 20 for border #1)
Make 71 sashing and
cornerstone units

ASSEMBLY DIAGRAM

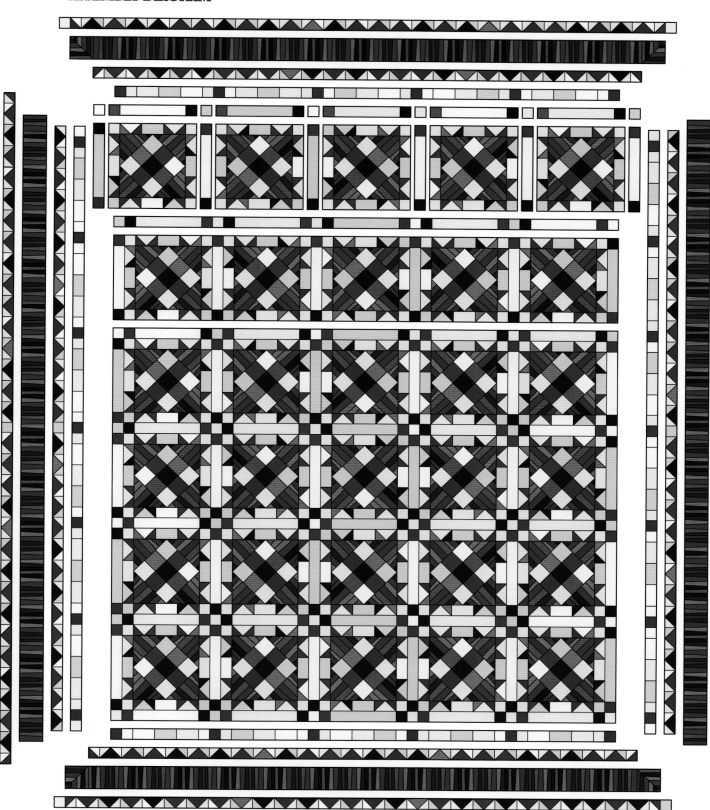

Tulip Fields

QUILT SIZE: 76″ x 84″

BLOCK SIZE: 7″ FINISHED

Small strings and crumbs are precious pieces and so much can be done with them! Even small units can be a place to show off your little bits. The base units for these tulip blocks are string pieced, and added to the patchwork parts to complete each "flower." Solid red makes the tulips pop with color!

Fabric Requirements

2 ¼ yards solid red for tulip tips and cornerstones

4 yards assorted neutral scraps for tulip backgrounds and block sashings

3 yards assorted colored scraps and strings for tulip bases and string pieced border

1 ½ yards cheddar print for sashing

½ yard black stripe for inner border

Tulip Bases

Following directions for string blocks on pages 6-9, prepare 144 – 4″ paper foundation squares for blocks and 80 – 4 ½″ foundations squares for the string border. Set border foundations aside for later use.

Note: It is helpful to start with a 1 ½″ to 2″ strip placed on the center diagonal of your block since we will be sub-cutting these blocks down the center diagonal.

Add strips to either side of the center strip until the foundation is completely covered. I prefer to use at least 5 pieces per block. Most of my tulip bases in this quilt have 3 string pieces, but some have more, showing 4 or 5 pieces. Press as you sew. Square units to 3 ⅞″ square. Make 144.

Diagrams are on page 78-79.

A

Slice blocks on the diagonal through the center string, yielding 2 tulip base triangles from each string block Remove the paper from the string triangles. Make 288 tulip base triangles.

Tulip Tops

From neutral scraps cut 288 – 2″ squares for block corners.

From neutral scraps cut 144 – 2 ¾″ squares for tulip tip triangles.

From solid red cut 144 – 2 ¾″ squares for tulip tip triangles.

Lay red 2 ¾″ squares with neutral 2 ¾″ squares with right sides together. Slice these corner to corner across the diagonal in both directions with an X to yield 4 quarter square triangle pairs. Repeat the process, dividing pairs into two equal groups.

B

Stitch 288 pairs with red on the right, and 288 pairs in mirror image with red on the left. It is important to pay attention to which side of the pair the red goes.

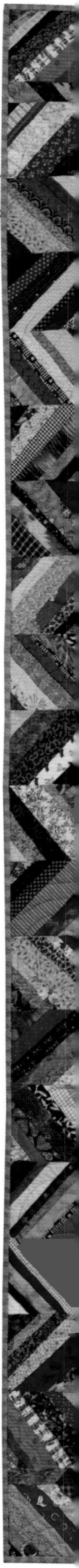

C

Join these units to two sides of the block corner squares as shown to create 288 tulip tops. Press seams to one side.

D

Add a tulip base to each of these units. Press to the base. Make 288. Units should measure 3 ½″ unfinished and 3″ finished.

Block Assembly

From neutral scraps, cut 288 – 1 ½″ x 3 ½″ sashing

From solid red, cut 162 – 1 ½″ squares. 72 are for block centers and 90 are for the cornerstones

E

Lay out block units as shown with sashing and block centers. Sew block into rows and join rows to complete each block. Make 72 blocks.

Quilt Top Assembly

From the cheddar print cut 161 – 1 ½″ x 7 ½″ sashing strips.

Referring to the Quilt Assembly Diagram on page 81 lay out the blocks in rows along with the sashing and cornerstones. Stitch the quilt center into rows, pressing seams toward the sashing, and away from the cornerstones. Join the rows to complete the quilt center.

Borders

Inner Border

Cut 8 – 1 ½″ strips across the width of the fabric from selvage to selvage. Join the 8 border strips end to end with diagonal seams to make a strip approximately 320″ long. Trim excess ¼″ from seams and press seams open.

Lay the quilt center out on the floor, smoothing it gently. Do not tug or pull. Measure the quilt through the center from top to bottom. Cut two inner side borders this length. Sew the inner side borders to the quilt sides with right sides together, pinning to match centers and ends. Ease where necessary to fit. Press seams toward the borders.

Repeat for top and bottom inner borders, measuring across the quilt center, including the borders just added in the measurement. Cut top and bottom inner borders this length. Stitch the top and bottom inner borders to the quilt center, pinning to match centers and ends, easing where necessary to fit. Press seams toward borders.

Outer Border

Following string piecing directions on pages 6-9, cover the 80 – 4 ½″ border foundations cut previously with diagonal strings. Trim blocks to 4 ½″ square. Remove paper foundations.

Note: Borders will be pieced long, and ends trimmed to fit your own quilt measurements.

Side borders: Stitch 20 blocks side by side in zigzag fashion into one long length.

Top/Bottom borders

Stitch 18 blocks side by side in zigzag fashion into one long length.

4 blocks are saved for corners.

Lay the quilt center out on the floor, smoothing it gently. Do not tug or pull. Find the center of the top, and lay a side border across the quilt from top to bottom, matching the center seam of the border with the center of the quilt. I find it helps if I stick some pins through the quilt top and into the carpet to anchor it.

Leave the excess extending beyond the quilt top and bottom, smoothing the border against the top center. Trim the excess border that hangs beyond the quilt at top and bottom. Repeat for remaining side border.

Now do the same thing with the quilt top and bottom borders, laying them across the quilt center, matching the center of each border with the center of the quilt, and letting equal amounts of excess extend beyond the quilt sides. Trim the excess border from both ends of the top and bottom borders.

Sew the side borders to the quilt sides with right sides together, pinning to match centers and ends, watching placement for the center "V" of the string border on each side of the quilt. These should mirror each other in direction. Ease where necessary to fit. Press seams toward the borders.

Following placement in quilt assembly diagram, stitch a corner block to each end of the top and bottom borders, watching which way the strings fall. Stitch the top and bottom inner borders to the quilt center, pinning to match centers and ends, easing where necessary to fit. Press seams toward borders.

Finishing

Tulip Fields was machine quilted in antique gold thread with an edge-to-edge Baptist Fan design. A lime green binding completes the quilt, while punching up the colors found inside.

Tulip Fields
Directions At-A-Glance

A

TULIP BASES
Make 144 – 4″ string blocks. Square to 3 ⅞″ and cut in half on the diagonal through the center. Make 288 bases

B

MIRROR IMAGE PIECED TRIANGLES
Make 288 each

C

PIECED TULIP TOP
Make 288

D

TULIP UNIT
3 ½″ unfinished
Make 288

E

TULIP BLOCK
7 ½″ unfinished
Make 72

ASSEMBLY DIAGRAM

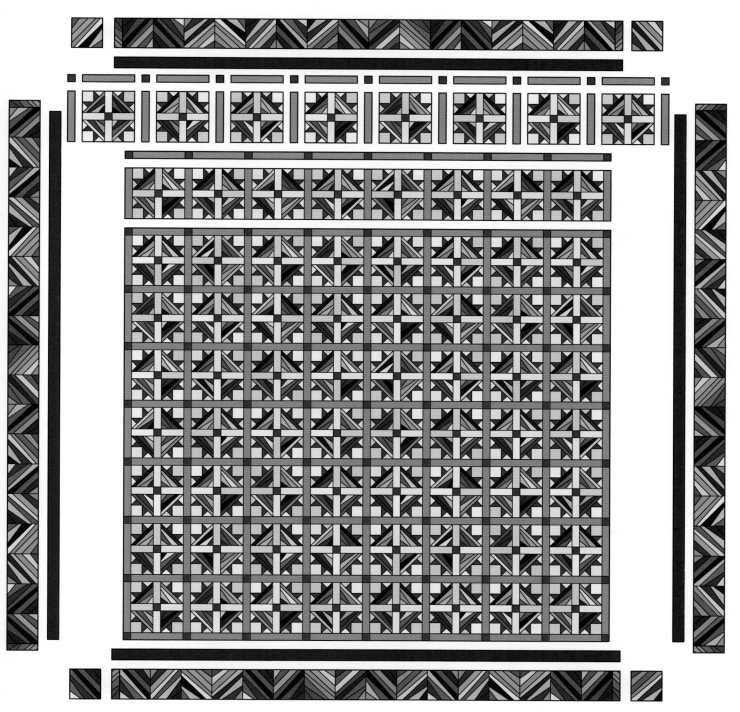

Wild Child

FINISHED QUILT SIZE: 77″ x 93″

FINISHED BLOCK SIZE: 8″

Blocks with large centers are the perfect spot to show off a wild variety of strings! You'll find everything in this quilt, perhaps even the proverbial "kitchen sink!"

Half the blocks have a cooling turquoise background, adding an "alternate block" look to this quilt, though all the blocks are identical – only the background colors have changed. Blocks are rotated to change the direction the strings lean and create a secondary design. A wild and modern floral border plays upon the myriad of color found in the quilt center.

I hadn't decided on a name for this quilt, but was leaning toward Wild Child, and while I was typing up the directions, "Wild Child" as sung by Enya just happened to come through the playlist on my iPod confirming my decision. Serendipity, indeed!

Fabric Requirements

2 ½ yards of neutral/light scraps for block backgrounds

3 yards of turquoise solid for block backgrounds and binding

4 yards of scraps and strings

½ yard red/white polka dot for the inner border

1 ¼ yards bold floral print for the outer border

String Centers

Following the directions for string blocks on pages 6-9, prepare 80 – 4 ½″ paper foundation squares.

Diagrams are on pages 84-85.

A

Using your scraps and strings, lay two strips right sides together across the center diagonal of the foundation square. Sew together and press. Continue until the paper base is completely covered. Square units to 4 ½″ and remove the paper. Make 80.

Half-Square Triangles

I used the Easy Angle Ruler and 2 ½″ strips from my scraps to cut the triangles used for this quilt. The traditional method of using 2 ⅞″ squares is given for those who do not have access to this ruler. Please see section on Using Specialty Rulers found on pages 94-95. You can use any method that gives you a 2 ½″ unfinished half-square triangle unit that finishes at 2″.

From the dark scraps cut 400 – 2 ⅞″ squares.

From the light scraps cut 200 – 2 ⅞″ squares.

From the turquoise solid cut 200 – 2 ⅞″ squares

B

Layer the dark squares and light squares with right sides together. Cut from corner to corner once on the diagonal to yield 400 matched pairs. Stitch into 400 half-square triangle units. Press to the dark and trim the dog ears. Each block requires 10 of these scrappy triangle units.

Repeat this process, matching the 200 turquoise squares with the 200 remaining dark scrap squares. Cut from corner to corner once on the diagonal to yield 400 matched pairs. Stitch into 400 half-square triangle units, enough for the remaining 40 blocks. Press to the dark and trim the dog ears. Each turquoise block requires 10 of these triangle units.

Side Sections

C

Make 80 neutral side section units by stitching two triangles with neutral backgrounds together as shown, playing close attention to the direction the triangles are facing.

Repeat with turquoise units, making 80 side section units.

D

Stitch side sections to string blocks as shown. Press seams toward string pieced centers. Note the direction the strings are laying, and keep them all in the same orientation. The blocks are identical in placement.

Top and Bottom Sections

From the neutral scraps, cut 80 - 2 ½″ squares

From the turquoise scraps, cut 80 - 2 ½″ squares

E

Stitch 3 neutral neutral half-square triangles end to end, paying close attention to which way the triangles are facing. Add neutral end square. Press. Make 80.

Stitch 3 turquoise neutral half-square triangles end to end, paying close attention to which way the triangles are facing. Add turquoise end square. Press. Make 80.

F

Join the top and bottom sections to the blocks. Press seams toward string pieced centers.

Layout

Referring to the Quilt Assembly Diagram, lay out the blocks in rows with 8 blocks across and 10 blocks down as shown. Notice that the turquoise blocks face one direction, and the neutral blocks are turned to complete the design. Study the quilt layout close enough and you will see stars appearing! Stitch the quilt center into rows. Join the rows to complete the quilt center.

Borders

Inner Border

Cut 8 – 2″ strips across the width of the fabric from selvage to selvage. Join the 8 border strips end to end with diagonal seams to make a strip approximately 320″ long. Trim excess ¼″ from seams and press seams open.

Lay the quilt center out on the floor, smoothing it gently. Do not tug or pull. Measure the quilt through the center from top to bottom. Cut two inner side borders this length. Sew the inner side borders to the quilt sides with right sides together, pinning to match centers and ends. Ease where necessary to fit. Press seams toward the borders.

Repeat for top and bottom inner borders, measuring across the quilt center, including the borders just added in the measurement. Cut top and bottom inner borders this length. Stitch the top and bottom inner borders to the quilt center, pinning to match centers and ends, easing where necessary to fit. Press seams toward borders.

Outer Border

From red print, cut 8 – 5″ strips across the width of the fabric from selvage to selvage. Join the 8 border strips end to end on the straight of grain to make a strip approximately 320″ long. Press seams open.

Add the outer borders in the same manner as the inner borders were added.

Finishing

Wild Child was machine quilted in turquoise thread with an edge-to-edge design called Check and Chase by Hermione Agee of Lorien Quilting, Australia. Refer to the resources page for contact information. A turquoise binding finishes everything just right!

Wild Child

Directions At-A-Glance

A

STRING CENTER
4 ½″ unfinished
Make 80

B

HALF-SQUARE TRIANGLE UNITS
2 ½″ unfinished
Make 400 dark/light
AND 400 dark/turquoise

C

NEUTRAL BLOCK SIDE SECTION
(shown left)
TURQUOISE BLOCK SIDE SECTION
(shown right)
Make 80 each

D

BLOCK WITH SIDE SECTIONS
Make 40 each

E

NEUTRAL BLOCK
(shown left)
TURQUOISE BLOCK
(shown right)
Make 80 each

F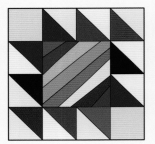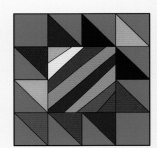

NEUTRAL BLOCK
(shown left)
TURQUOISE BLOCK
(shown right)
8 ½″ unfinished
Make 40 each

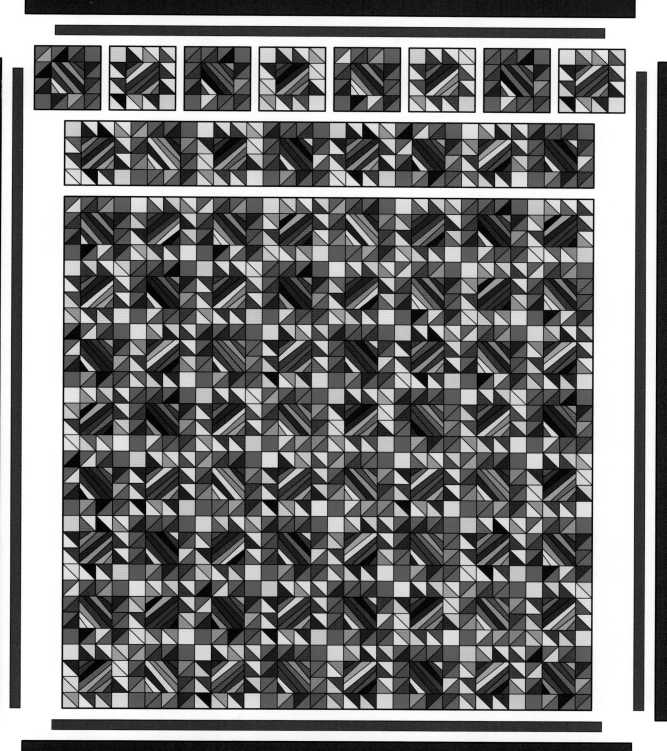

Zuckerwatte
(Cotton Candy)

FINISHED QUILT SIZE:
APPROXIMATELY 60″ x 72″

BLOCK SIZE: 6″ FINISHED

Recently, I spent quite a bit of time organizing my scraps and strings, which meant copious amounts of chick-flick movies on TV, and dumping out my string bins to divide them by color family. With this activity I realized many things – first, just how many strings a large bin can hold, and second, which colors were the most plentiful! This also gave me the push to use some of these overly abundant color families in scrappy string quilts.

Zuckerwatte is the German name for cotton candy, and doesn't this quilt just scream cotton candy? A real sweet treat in shades of pink and purple. Blocks are composed of pink and neutral string pieced units combined with half-square triangles that bring a lot of motion! A gently scalloped border and binding adds a soft touch, perfect for any girly-girl in your world!

Fabric Requirements

4 ½ yards of pink scraps and strings for blocks and outer border. Include prints, geometrics, florals, plaids and novelties

3 ½ yards of neutral/light scraps and strings for blocks. Include a wide variety of prints, stripes, plaids and geometrics ranging from white to cream to beige to tan. May include small figures, leaves and flowers as long as the fabric ground reads as neutral.

1 yard of purple scraps for half-square triangles

½ yard purple stripe for inner border

28″ square of purple for binding

Additional Requirements

Chalk pencil

Template plastic

Half-square triangle units

I used my Easy Angle ruler and 2 ½″ strips to make the half-square triangles for this quilt. The traditional method of cutting 2 ⅞″ squares is given for those who don't have access to this ruler. You can use any method that gives you 2″ finished half-square triangles.

From pink and purple scraps cut 120 – 2 ⅞″ squares.

From neutral scraps cut 120 – 2 ⅞″ squares.

Diagrams are on page 91-93.

A

Match neutral squares to the pink squares with right sides together, and slice from corner to corner on the diagonal, yielding 240 pink/neutral triangle pairs. Stitch these with a ¼″ seam allowance and press to the dark. Trim dog ears. Make 240. Units measure 2 ½″ unfinished and 2″ finished.

Single triangles

From pink and purple scraps cut 80 – 2 ⅞″ squares, cut in half on the diagonal.

From neutral scraps cut 80 – 2 ⅞″ squares, cut in half on the diagonal.

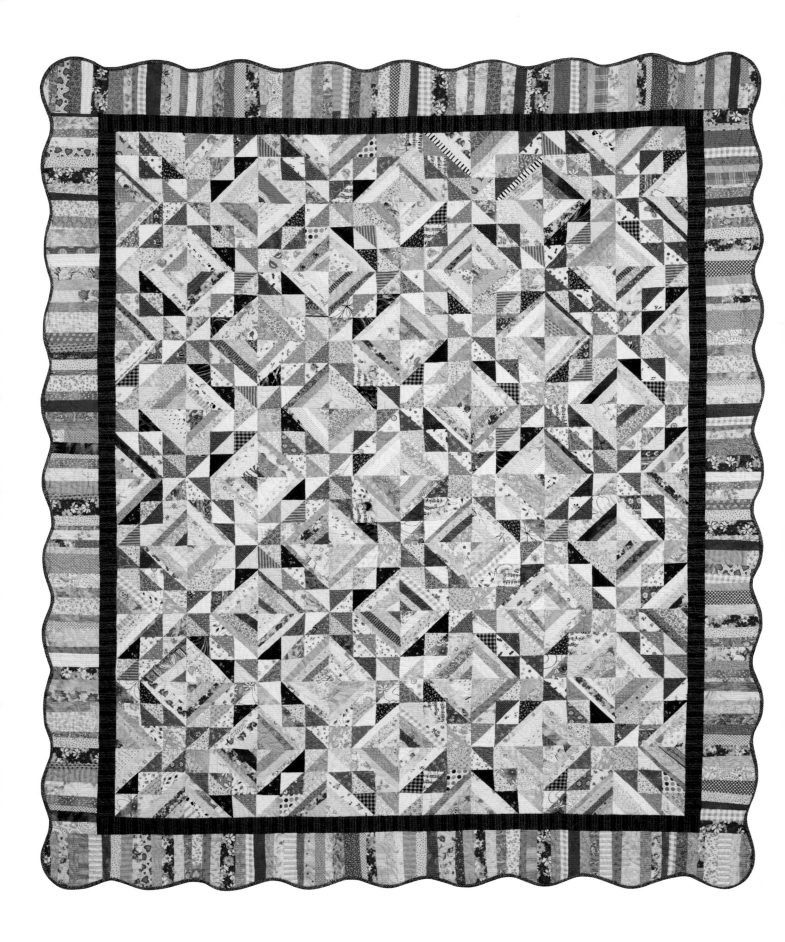

Block center assembly

B

Sew a half-square triangle unit to a pink or purple single triangle. Press to the triangle.

C

Sew a neutral single triangle to the left of a half-square triangle unit. Press to the triangle. Sew a pink or purple single triangle to the right of the half-square triangle unit. Press to the triangle.

D

Sew a neutral triangle to the left of a half-square triangle unit. Press to the triangle.

E

Stitch the rows together to make 80 center sections

String Units

Following the directions for string blocks on pages 6-9, prepare 80 – 5″ foundation squares.

Note: It is helpful to start with a 2″ strip down the center diagonal of your block since we will be sub-cutting these blocks down the center diagonal.

Using your neutral strings, add strips to either side of the center strip until the foundation is completely covered. Press as you sew. Square units to 4 ⅞″. Make 40.

Using your pink strings, add strips to either side of the center strip until the foundation is completely covered. Press as you sew. Square units to 4 ⅞″. Make 40.

F

Slice the blocks from corner to corner through the center strip and remove the paper.

Block Assembly

G

Add one pink string triangle to the pink side of the block center and a neutral string triangle to the purple side. Press toward the string triangles. Make 80 blocks.

Referring to the Quilt Assembly Diagram on page 95, lay out blocks as shown, with 8 blocks across and 10 blocks down. Stitch blocks into rows, and join rows to complete quilt center. Press block seams in opposing directions so they will nest when joining the rows.

Borders

Inner Border

From the dark purple stripe, cut 7 – 2″ strips x the width of fabric.

Join the strips end to end with diagonal seams to create one long length, measuring approximately 280″. Trim the excess ¼″ beyond seams. Press the seams open.

Lay quilt out on the floor, smoothing it gently. Do not tug or pull. Measure the quilt through the center from top to bottom and cut two inner side borders this length. Sew inner side borders to the quilt sides with right sides together, pinning to match centers and ends. Ease where necessary to fit. Press seams to the borders.

Repeat steps for top and bottom inner borders, measuring across the width of the quilt including the borders just added. Cut top and bottom inner borders this length. Sew to quilt top and bottom with right sides together, pinning to match centers and ends. Ease where necessary to fit. Press seams to the borders.

String Pieced Outer Border

Cover 15 sheets of 8 ½″ x 11″ paper with pink strings. Place the strings straight on the LENGTH down the center of the page (not diagonal). I like to use reject printer paper for this step, as it is bigger than phone book pages, and I can get more coverage.

When the page is covered, trim it to 8 ½″ x 11″. Using a ruler, cut two 5 ½″ widths ACROSS the strings from side to side across the paper. Each piece of covered paper will yield 2 border units. Remove the paper. Join border units end to end into one long length.

Lay out the quilt on the floor, smoothing it gently and measure the quilt through the center from top to bottom. Cut two outer side borders this length. Sew outer side borders to quilt sides with right sides together, pinning to match centers and ends. Ease where necessary to fit. Press seams toward the inner border.

Repeat for top and bottom outer borders, measuring across the quilt center and including the borders just added in the measurement. Stitch top and bottom outer borders to quilt center, pinning to match centers and ends, easing where necessary. Press seams toward the inner border.

Quilting

Quilt edges are gently scalloped and bound with bias binding after the quilting is finished. **Zuckerwatte** is machine quilted in pink thread using a four-petal flower design called Lavish by Hermione Agee of Lorien Quilting, Australia. Refer to the resources page for contact information. A gentle scalloped binding completes the quilt, adding a delicate touch to a riot of scraps!

To add a gently curved binding to the quilt, trace the border templates found on page 93 on to template plastic and cut out along traced lines. Using a chalk pencil, trace around the templates to mark the scallops on the outer border. Mark the corners first, and use the side template from the quilt corner in toward the center of the border, adjusting the spacing as necessary. Do not cut the scallops now. This will be done after the binding is attached.

Bias Binding

Cut a 28″ square of binding fabric. Cut square in half diagonally from corner to corner into 2 triangles. With right sides together, rearrange and sew the straight grain of the triangles together into a large diamond.

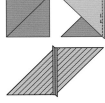

Draw lines 2″ apart on the wrong side of the fabric along the bias edge as shown. Cut off any remaining fabric less than this width as you reach the end of the parallelogram.

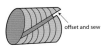

offset and sew

Make a tube by bringing the right sides of the fabric together offsetting the ends by one line, and still having the lines match each other exactly down the seam. Sew the ends together with a ¼″ seam and press the seam open.

Start cutting at one end of the tube, cutting along the line and opening the tube up into one long length of binding. Bring the wrong sides and raw edges together, and carefully press bias strip in half lengthwise to complete binding preparation. Square off ends of binding.

On the Flip Side

Even the back holds a surprise! A bunch of orphan blocks containing pink, purple, lime green and blue came together to make the quilt back as fun as the front.

Attaching the Binding

The binding will be attached before trimming the edges of the quilt to keep the border flat and to prevent puckers.

Beginning at the high point of one side scallop, match raw edges of binding to drawn scallop line on the quilt border. Stitch ¼″ from raw edge of binding, leaving a 4″ tail of binding unsewn at the beginning for joining later. Go slowly, repositioning quilt and binding only a few inches ahead of where you are sewing, gently easing binding around the curves, pinning as needed, keeping the binding as smooth as possible. Do not stretch binding.

Continue sewing the binding around the quilt stopping 6″ to 8″ short from where you started. Overlap the ends of the binding and trim the end tail ½″ PAST the beginning of the start tail. Strips will overlap ½″. Open out the strips, stitch them end to end with right sides together with a ¼″ seam and press the seam open. Fold the binding back in half, and complete the last few inches of stitching the binding to the quilt top.

Trim the quilt top, batting and backing ¼″ from stitching line, even with the raw edges of the binding.

To finish, fold the binding over the edge of the quilt and blind-stitch the binding to the backing just past the seam line.

Zuckerwatte
Directions At-A-Glance

A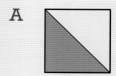

HALF-SQUARE TRIANGLE UNITS
2 ½″ unfinished
Make 240

B

ROW 1
Make 80

C

ROW 2
Make 80

D

ROW 3
Make 80

E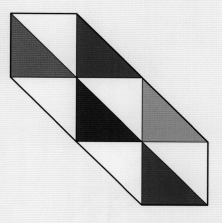

BLOCK CENTER
Make 80.

F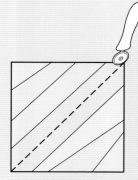

STRING TRIANGLE UNITS
Make 40 neutral
Make 40 pink

G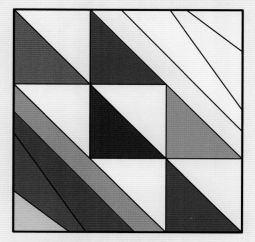

ZUCKERWATTE BLOCK
6 ½″ unfinished
Make 80

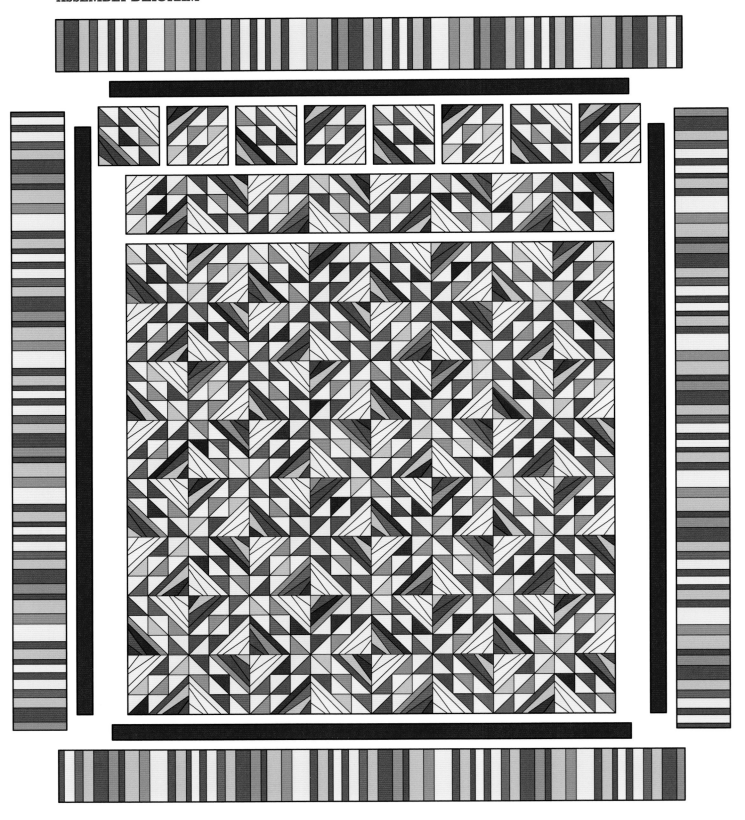

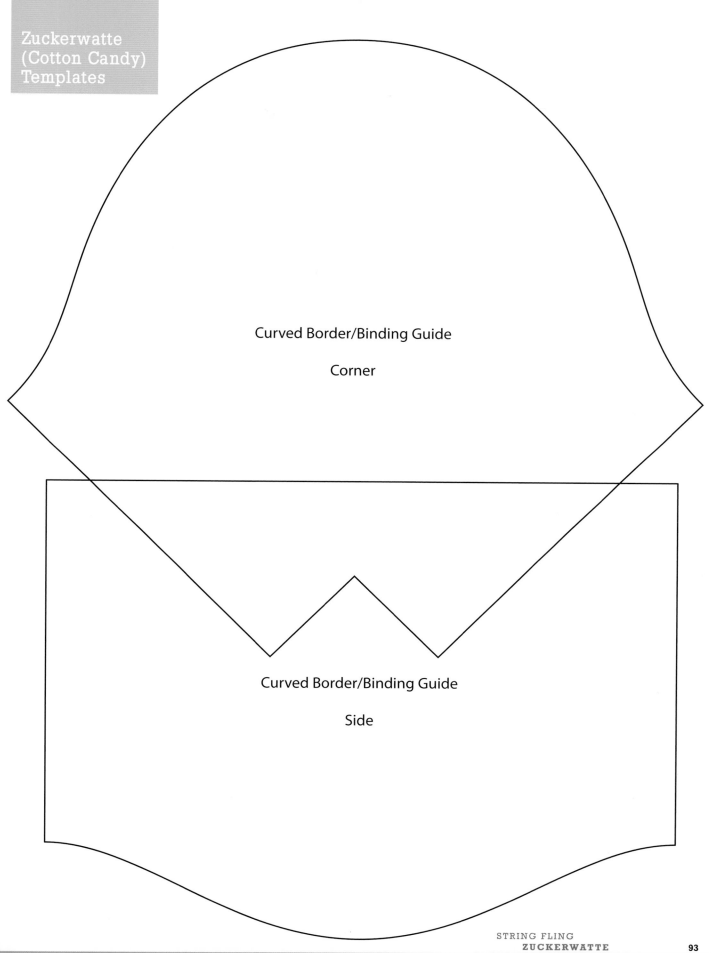

Curved Border/Binding Guide

Corner

Curved Border/Binding Guide

Side

Using Specialty Rulers

This book on making scraps quilting wouldn't be complete without listing some of my favorite tools. I am in no way affiliated with any of the companies who produce these rulers. I just love their products. There are many ruler manufacturers out there – you might find you like one kind better than another. These are a sampling of my favorites.

Note: The resources section (below) lists more information on these companies and how to access step-by-step tutorials on how to use the rulers.

6 ½″ x 12 ½″ rotary ruler by Creative Grids

I find this ruler to be the best size for just about everything. I like that there is no color other than black and white. And the lines are thin enough that I don't have to guess where the edge of my fabric is underneath that line.

Sometimes rulers have so many markings that it is hard to find just the line you need. Since my scraps are cut and sorted in ½ inch increments, most of the time I don't need ³/₈″ or ⁷/₈″ lines. And as I get older, my eyesight gets more persnickety!

Easy Square and Easy Square Jr.
by EZ Quilting

For smaller cuts I use the **Easy Square Jr.** It has only ¼″ markings and ½″ markings. I like the dotted ¼″ line all the way around the square. I use this one when trimming blocks. It's great for paper piecing because I can put the dotted line on the line on the paper, and trim ¼″ past it. It's also great for cutting smaller scraps into squares and bricks without having to use a huge ruler.

The 9-½″ **Easy Square** is great for squaring up larger blocks. Two sides have that ¼″ seam allowance marked so I can be sure not to trim off points.

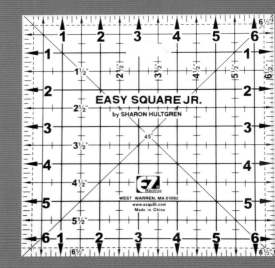

Easy Square and Easy Square Jr.
by EZ Quilting

Resources

Specialty Rulers

EZ Quilting by Wrights
(800) 660-0415
Email: help@wrights.com
Web: www.ezquilt.com

Creative Grids USA
400 W. Dussel Dr.
Maumee, OH 43537
(419) 893-3636
Web: www.creativegridsusa.com

Quilting Designs

Patricia E Ritter, Urban Elementz
125 Sunny Creek
New Braunfels, TX 78132
(830) 964-6133
Email: patricia@urbanelementz.com
Web: www.urbanelementz.com

Hermoine Agee, Lorien Quilting
30 Lockwood Rd,
Belgrave Heights 3160 VIC Australia
Phone: (03) 9754 4916
Email: hermione@lorienquilting.com
Web: www.lorienquilting.com

Jodi Beamish, Willow Leaf Studio
(888) 945-5695
Email: wlscontact@gmail.com
Web: www.willowleafstudio.com
www.digiquilter.com

Georgette Dell'Orco, Quilter's Niche
Phone: (619) 663-0320
Email: info@quiltersniche.com
Web: http://www.quiltersniche.com

Jessica Schick, Digi-tech
Phone: 715-831-1126
Email: jessica@digitechpatterns.com
Web: www.digitechpatterns.com

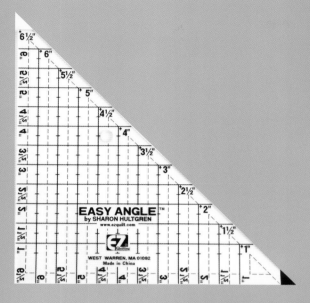

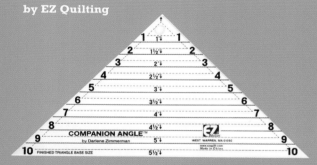

Easy Angle and
Companion Angle
by EZ Quilting

Easy Angle and Companion Angle
by EZ Quilting

I use the **Easy Angle** ruler to cut half-square triangle units from strips without having to add that ⅞″ to the finished size! You just add ½″ to the finished size of the unit to cut your strip, and the rest of the math is added in for you on the angled side. Cut matched sets with your strips right sides together and you are ready to just feed the half-square triangle pairs through your machine. This works great with my scrap strips, because I don't have that ⅞″ to worry about.

The **Companion Angle**, when used with the **Easy Angle**, can make a number of units that I use most often including the "goose" part of flying geese units and "hour glass" units. It also works anywhere else I want the straight of grain to be on the longest side of the triangle. This versatile ruler also works with strips in the sizes I already keep on hand.

Bonnie K. Hunter is passionate about quiltmaking, focusing mainly on scrap quilts with the simple feeling of "making do." She started her love affair with quilting in a home economics class her senior year of high school. Before quilting became her full time career, Bonnie was the owner and designer of Needle in a Haystack!! creating more than 70 patterns for dolls and stuffed animals with a country primitive feel.

About The Author

Many of her designs were licensed through the Butterick Pattern Company, translated into seven languages and sold around the globe through fabric stores. But quilting has always been Bonnie's first love. She has been machine quilting since 1989 and professionally long arm quilting for the public since 1995, retiring in 2009 when she no longer had the time due to her teaching, traveling and writing schedule. She has been featured in magazines both for her quilt patterns and articles she has written on scrap management and using that stash to its full potential.

Dedicated to continuing the traditions of quilting, Bonnie enjoys meeting with quilters, teaching workshops and lecturing to quilt guilds all over the world, challenging quilters to break the rules, think outside the box, and find what brings them joy. (Bonnie received the 2011 "Teacher of the Year" award through a global internet poll hosted via Sew Cal Gal, and was completely flabbergasted, not to mention honored and humbled at the same time.)

When not traveling and teaching, she spends her time piecing scrap quilts, enjoying the peaceful reward of English paper piecing and hand quilting as much as machine work, and loving life in her wooded surroundings in beautiful rural Wallburg, North Carolina, a suburb of Winston-Salem. She and her husband, Dave, are the proud parents of two grown sons, Jason and Jeffrey. They round out their household with Sadie the dog and two cats – Emmy Lou, who loves life inside only, and Chloe who only loves life on the outside – keeping Bonnie company while she designs, quilts and plays happily with her fabric.

Bonnie also writes a regular column for *Quiltmaker* magazine entitled "Addicted to Scraps" with the main intention to help you to put various aspects of your own Scrap Users System to good use!

Catch up with Bonnie's doings through her extensive website at www.Quiltville.com. There you will find Quiltville's calendar for lectures and workshops, tips and tricks, techniques, tutorials and a long list of free quilt patterns to help you dig into your scraps.

From there, head over to Quiltville.blogspot.com for Bonnie's (almost) daily blog, Quiltville's Quips & Snips. Her global email list, Quiltvillechat, found at groups.yahoo.com/group/quiltvillechat/ has become a hot spot for mystery quilters from all over the world with a focus on using scraps and stash.

Don't forget Facebook! Keep in real-time touch with Bonnie on the Quiltville Friends Page.

Bonnie's favorite motto? "The Best Things in Life are Quilted!!" of course!